SOUTHERN VAPORS

SOUTHERN VAPORS

LYNN GARSON

While this is a memoir, and family members and events are described to the best of my recollection, I recognize that others' memories of the people and events described may be different than my own. Except for me, the characters are an amalgamation of real people, fictional constructs, wishful thinking, moments of playfulness, projection, middle-aged memory, temporary insanity and not-so-temporary insanity. I, on the other hand, am real and this is my story.

To my children

I hope you dance.

CONTENTS

PART ONE: HELP

PART TWO: SHAPING SUZY

PART THREE: QUEST

PART FOUR: THE ART OF LIVING

PART FIVE: RUN FOR THE ROSES

PART ONE

HELP

CHAPTER ONE

A STRONG CASE OF THE VAPORS

WHEN I HAD MY FIRST ultra deluxe, super king size fit of the vapors in March of 2000, I had been spiraling down for months and was ingesting food like other people mainlined drugs. I interviewed for a program at an eating disorders clinic on a Friday and was "invited" to join as an inpatient the following Monday. That morning in the parking lot was the first time I thought about what the program would be like. As a novice to the rehab scene, I thought that maybe it would be a combination of Weight Watchers and Overeaters

Anonymous—some support mixed with recipes and food plans.

I crossed the parking lot, walked through the door and left it to swing closed behind me. The door slammed shut instead, locking audibly and with finality. As out of it as I was, something shifted in my awareness, like sensing a big cat moving in my shadow. I walked down the hall and my eyes settled on a girl, maybe eighteen years old, sitting in a wheel chair with a feeding tube coming out of her arm. I had never seen anyone that thin in real life, only in pictures from concentration camps. Thus began my real education, and I had to wonder what had brought me to the point that I needed that particular kind of lesson.

As a child, I had been extraordinarily sheltered, existing in my small world like a butterfly in a cocoon, raised in a big white-columned house by the river, devoting much of my spare time to reading Victorian novels spiced with a dash of Harlequin romance. It was in those pages that I first learned about "the vapors," but it was a number of years before I realized that I was similarly afflicted, and many more years after that until I understood the reality of what that meant, as so aptly brought to life by a friend who had a way with words: "the inability, when faced with calamity as a grown woman, to pull up your big girl panties." I grew up in Atlanta in the 1960s but had only been downtown once before the age of twenty-one, to see *Gone with the*

Wind as an eight-year-old. I had never ridden a bus before college, never babysat, never even held a baby until the age of thirty. I was taught how to drive (badly) by the family chauffeur, shifting the "three on the tree" manual gear shift into second gear at a bone jarring ten miles per hour, if that.

So my visit to the eating disorder clinic turned my world upside down in a multitude of ways, from that first vision of a starving teenager to the final session at the end of my third week, which left me with an indelible memory. There was a young woman in her early twenties at the clinic whose mother would come to visit at family sessions. The daughter was anorexic, and most recently had suffered a heart attack and been hospitalized, near death. At the family session on my last day, the mother declared, in her daughter's presence, "I don't care anymore. I have gone through the treatments, the upswings, the downswings and the hospitalizations too many times, and I can't do it anymore. You may die, but I have another child that I have to be there for, and this is unfair and I have done as much as I can for you."

I had three children myself at the time, and was both appalled and bewildered that a mother could say such a thing. I wondered how that young woman felt (she gave no sign of her feelings after her mother spoke), and thought how unutterably alone I would have felt in her place. The daughter was such a creative person, forever beading hairpins, one of which I still keep in my jewelry box. I wondered about the relationship between that mother and daughter in earlier days, before the disease came into play. It took me back to my younger days, so confusing and hard to navigate, despite trappings that others thought made for a life free of care.

CHAPTER TWO

MY LIFE AS A PRINCESS

H OW MANY PEOPLE GROW UP in a house that really does look like Tara, with servants who "come with the property"? Since the publication of the book *The Help* by Kathryn Stockett, presumably it is politically correct to talk about these things without risking being thought a bigot, which I am not. Strikingly for the times, my Northern mother taught me to be colorblind, and as a child I took baths with my black nursemaid's daughter and spent almost as much time at her family's AME

(African Methodist Episcopal) church as I did at our synagogue.

My parents purchased the home where I grew up in 1952, the year before I was born. It was the only home I ever knew, and what seemed like luxuries to others were just part of the landscape to me. There was a log cabin on the grounds inhabited by a woman employed by the previous owners as their laundress. Her husband lived there with her, an ancient, toothless soul who collected brown eggs from our chickens. Willie Sue and James really did come with the property: they stayed in the cabin with its pot-belly stove and came to work for my family, a seamless transition. Willie Sue wore a kerchief around her head every day except Sunday and scrubbed the clothes on a washboard for most of my youth. She carried a switch and applied it equally and liberally to our four dogs and me and my brother.

James died when I was very young, but Willie Sue worked for my family for decades, washing, ironing and neatly folding everything from my shirts to my underwear, then passing it up the chain of the household staff for distribution. I still react to ironed and folded underwear (courtesy of someone other than myself) the way other people react to milk and cookies—suffused with feelings of warmth and light and being cared for.

Long after I was grown and out of the house, Willie Sue finally moved up North to retire with family. The log cabin fell into disrepair, but I went in once years later while I could still get through the tangled ivy that choked the hill in front. There was dust everywhere, blanketing rickety furniture and a couple of brown bottles sitting on the table. I suppose that there are any numbers of houses like that decaying throughout the South. Some day I would like to take a trip across the United States, photographing the old sheds and houses in their various stages of decay, trying to tease the stories of their inhabitants from the remnants they left behind.

At the same time that Willie Sue and James worked for us, we had Amelia and George, she my nursemaid and the principal housemaid, he the chauffeur, butler and all- around handyman. They lived in the "servants' quarters" off the kitchen with their daughter, Pamela. I won't go so far as to say that my brother and I were raised by Amelia and George, but for my part, they certainly had as much impact on my life as my parents from birth to age thirteen.

My mother referred to George fondly as the "perfect servant," trained as he was by the U.S. Navy. He was also an alcoholic, not a mean drunk I am told, but from stories I gather that it made him, on occasion, unreliable. One time my parents came back from six weeks in Europe to find George passed out in the back yard and everyone else missing (I was four, my brother ten).

Amelia showed up with us hours later—she had been worried about George's drinking and gotten us the hell out of there. Did I mention that George kept a shotgun in his closet?

Amelia was kindness itself, constantly hugging me to her maternal bosom, bathing me and brushing my long hair dry before she braided it. She loved to tell me, in her high-pitched voice: "A woman's hair is her crowning glory." Amelia is the reason that I did not become more unbalanced than I did; she was the source of a measure of unconditional love in my life and provided a much-needed counterpoint to my mother's temper, which often was extreme.

Amelia and George's daughter, Pamela, was just a couple of years older than I, and I grew up with her as a sister, playing in the yard, running under the sprinklers, drinking the iron-spiked water. I'll never forget that taste; nothing ever tasted better. Although this was during the 1950s and '60s, I was completely unaware of race as an issue or of discrimination, never to my knowledge saw a segregated lunch counter or a sign at a water fountain. I did know that the "n" word was never to be spoken, period, and it still comes as a shock to me that in the twenty-first century it is acceptable slang among younger people in both the white and the African American communities. That I had no black friends in school says nothing for or against me since there weren't any black people in either of my schools, not one person in all of my twelve years of secondary education ending in 1971.

When I was thirteen years old, Amelia and George disappeared. They were at home when I left for school in the morning, and when I came home in the afternoon they were gone, no note, no nothing. They had been fired, but my mother rebuffed any effort on my part to ask why or how or what had happened. So I just swept it under the rug, thirteen years of my life and the people I loved disappearing in a puff of smoke.

My parents hired another couple after Amelia and George. She was the cook and he was again the butler/chauffeur, but they had nothing to do with raising me. Elias was an older black man, and his mindset was that of earlier times. Martin Luther King, Jr. might as well never have existed for all the faith that Elias put in racial equality.

One day Elias was driving me to school and a dog ran out in the road. Unavoidably, we hit him. To my shock, Elias started to drive on. I yelled, "Elias, stop the car, we have to get that dog and take him up the hill to the Pomerands!" (I knew whose dog it was; I had taken riding lessons with their daughter and she was ahead of me by a year in high school.) "Noam, noam, Miss Lynn, I can't, they gonc string me up!" "Elias, you can't leave this dog here! We've got to get him up to the house, he's still breathing and maybe they can get him to the vet!" "Noam, noam, Miss Lynn!!" He actually drove on a few yards before I convinced him to back up and take me up the hill so I could talk to the owners.

One thing I never forgot: the Pomerands weren't all that nice and I came away with a whiff, just a whiff, of what Elias' reality might have been.

At the same time that Elias and his wife worked for us we had a yardman named "Lester." My mother retrieved him from the bus stop one day and that was the beginning of a beautiful fifteen-year partnership. Other than the fact that Lester drank, and every so often my mother would have to cart him to the hospital where he would battle with the D.T.s, it was a match made in heaven. My mother and Lester worked in the vegetable plots, shoulder to shoulder, day after day, summer after summer. We had twenty-three acres inside the Atlanta city limits and my mother, with Lester's help, put a good portion of the land to use, with cornfields, vegetable plots, formal gardens, rose gardens and boxwood hedges. Those who till the land impress me to this day, retiring in defeat as I did after half a day one summer picking beans, hotter and more uncomfortable than I had ever been.

We also had our share of help who were "connected," which made me feel cool, adding unexpectedly to the distinction of my family. We had an upstairs maid (that in itself is notable), an anorexic-looking woman who seemed constantly unnerved, reminding me of one of our quivering greyhounds. She was aunt to several of the Pips, who sang backup to Gladys Knight, a Motown diva of the 1960s and '70s on the order of Aretha Franklin or Diana Ross. Gladys would send Vonna a plane ticket to Detroit every once in a while, and off she'd go, a broomstick wrapped up in a coat, to reappear on Monday morning in our driveway in her enormous Oldsmobile, creeping along. I don't think she knew that a car had an accelerator pedal.

We also employed a woman whose niece was a top political mover and shaker in Atlanta. I use the term "employed" loosely, because Emily had worked for my grandparents, and after their deaths moved over to my mother in a supervisory capacity. Her principal activity was to report to my mother on the doings of the rest of the help, particularly what Emily viewed as their frequent infractions. Emily had cooked traditional Jewish food for my grandmother in New York for years and would reprise it occasionally, serving up world-class gefilte fish and chopped liver.

All of us in my family were foodies, ranging from gourmands (my father, brother and me) to the lone gourmet (my mother). We loved our fried chicken in particular, expertly prepared in vats of Crisco, first by Odetta, then Amelia, and finally Elias' wife, Betty. One memorable evening we all agreed that Betty's chicken that night fell short of the high standard to which we had become accustomed, but no matter, we ate it anyway, only to find the next day that Elias had given her garden lime out of the pantry to coat the chicken instead of flour. If he did it on purpose it was pretty damned smart, and he had good reason to exact revenge where he could: he used to hide from my mother under the piano—that's how much she scared him. I saw him with my own eyes, crouched under the piano in the music room, shaking with fear. I also saw him once behind the living room sofa, but that time he was just asleep.

Fried chicken is weighted with memories for me. My brother and I weren't allowed to eat as much as we wanted at the dinner table for fear (my mother's, not ours) of gaining weight, so we learned how to slip down the back staircase to raid the refrigerator without being heard. I could have been an Indian scout, I got so good at testing the treads on the steps and avoiding the ones that creaked. There was always extra chicken for the help ("toting privileges" were an automatic employee benefit in those days). Whether they were happy to share with me and my brother I don't know, but share they did, and at least we saved them the bother of cleaning up, because we would take the bones, scoured clean, to the long attic behind the playroom, stand in the doorway and pitch them as far as we could into the blackness of the unlit room. When my parents sold the house decades later, I understand that there were molted snake skins in the attic; I guess the bones were a tasty treat for the snakes.

Besides the fried chicken, I was introduced by Amelia to Southern cuisine at its country best: squirrel and grits with squirrel gravy (very peppery), fried catfish, gutted fresh in the back sink, stewed rabbit, cornbread, collards and, the pièce de résistance, chitlins. These last had a horrific smell; they had to simmer on the stove for two solid days, so Amelia would take advantage of my parents' lengthy trips abroad to cook up a pot, and the house would stink for days. I haven't smelled chitlins for years, but I bet if I did, it would take me right back, just like boiled peanuts and watermelon and fried chicken gizzards (a family favorite, even to my gourmet mother).

It sounds good on paper: family dinners at 7:00 p.m. in our cozy breakfast room, all four dogs in attendance, the routine of school during fall, winter, and spring, and every day of the summer spent swimming with my friends at our club. I had nice clothes and nicer vacations. From the outside, the panorama was one of constancy and comfort. That was on the surface. Underneath I felt the tectonic plates shifting (Amelia's here; Amelia's gone?), and I lost my balance.

CHAPTER THREE

EARTHQUAKE

B Y THE TIME I was in college, my inability to cope was already a threat to my sanity, and depression lurked around the corner like a vulture. I spent a week of my first semester at Tulane in bed reading the entire James Bond series and eating candy bars. It took a concerted effort by my worried friends to pry me out.

Still, at that time I had long periods that were depression-free, and I made it through college and law school without too much turmoil, although close friends were aware of my tendencies. I had a friend in law school who said that I was like the heroine in one of the Victorian novels I still had the habit of reading, who lies on her chaise longue languidly fanning herself, unable to summon the energy to move. Then she finds out that she needs to go kill somebody. She gets up, gets the gun, goes and kills the person, comes back and lies back down on the chaise, one arm draped weakly over her face.

That friend knew me well. My particular affliction, until my later years when the bottom truly fell out, was always offset by a certain strength, a fail-safe mechanism that kicked in at the eleventh hour and prodded me to take whatever action was called for. That strength also allowed me to build a more than creditable life in my twenties and thirties—I became a lawyer, well-heeled, top 10% of my law school class, owner of businesses, citizen of Paris and Hong Kong, married and mother of three children. To anyone who did not know me intimately, I seemed at that time relentlessly competent, effortlessly secure, outgoing, even aggressive when circumstances demanded it.

The average person who came into contact with me was unaware of my hidden self, the persona whom I affectionately named "Suzy Marmalade." Suzy was the product of an improbable union— Suzy Creamcheese,[1] Frank Zappa's fictional groupie whose name had instant meaning for me, perfectly evoking a wide-eyed innocent, nonetheless endearing, and the psychedelic "marmalade skies" made famous by the Beatles,[2] everything edgy that I yearned to be but was not.

Suzy has always been the guardian of some of my most admirable traits, like compassion and kindness and loyalty. She is easy going and nonjudgmental, a staunch friend without a mean bone in her body. She is also gullible and naïve, and embodies the part of me that succumbs to the vapors, landing me in psychiatric institutions not once, not twice, but three times. The first was the eating disorder clinic in 2000, the second was the Cadillac of the rehab scene, which did a world-class but short-lived job of putting Humpty Dumpty back together again in 2008, and the third was a facility for drug addicts and criminals (which I am not now nor ever have been) that entertained me in 2010, doing little for my mental health but much for my knowledge of a world previously unimagined.

The earthquake hit in the winter of 2007. My decline that winter was notable for the contrast between how I felt and how I looked. In public, I put on a first-rate show. I closed two deals at work simultaneously while performing all of the regular mom duties during the weeks when I had custody of my daughter, Rachel (baking cookies, going to after-school sports, driving carpool when she had plans with her friends), planning my daughter Juliana's high school graduation weekend and attending various community events. I did it all if not with a smile on my face, then at least with a mask of propriety. No cracks were visible.

In private, I was suffering from an Olympian case of the vapors, and I spent most of my time either sobbing uncontrollably or prostrate— on my office floor, on psychiatrists' couches (all unaccountably prickly), on park benches, in my back yard and in my friends' arms. For six months I could not eat, sleep without pills or breathe without distress, and I exhibited the thousand-yard stare that is characteristic of soldiers devastated by war.

My symptoms sprang into life full-blown almost to the day when I decided to try to reconcile with my ex-husband, Leo. While my head thought it was a good idea, my body clearly disagreed, as did my two daughters, exhibiting far better sense than their mother. I consciously and deliberately ignored the part of myself that was frantically signaling that this was a mistake, ignored the internal arguments that raged. ("You can't do this, it's going to kill you." "Shut up, I am doing this, I don't care what you say.") I wanted my life and my home and my children back, and I didn't care what part of me I had to sacrifice to get it. The result was mental, emotional and physical scorched earth, and while my friends propped me up as best they could, it was a losing proposition. I was undergoing something quite beyond anyone's experience: it was like passing through the Eye of the Needle, being scoured to the bone, heated in a crucible and walking through the Valley of the Shadow of Death, except I did fear the Evil. When the miasma overtook me, it was from one instant to the next, like contracting the flu from an injection of a quick acting vaccine. The physical symptoms were bad—difficulty breathing, food turning to ashes in my mouth, sleeplessness, inability to concentrate, tunnel vision—but they were nothing compared to the psychological ones. The moment in the morning between sleep and wakefulness, when memory had yet to kick in and everything seemed okay, followed by a rushing awareness of everything falling apart. Living every moment like I was in an airplane that was plummeting to the ground, ruled by abject terror. Afraid for my life that none of this was ever going to change. My yoga teacher, one of those people who helped and still helps me to hold to the notion of a benevolent Universe, likened me to a sieve. I would come to her, leached of all faith, hope or belief, and she would fill me back up with encouragement, only for me to come back a few days later, psychologically and spiritually bereft, and we would repeat the lesson again, and again, and again.

I often regarded myself with disbelief during those days, when without warning I would fall to my knees, doubled over with grief, wracked with sobs that were more like howls, as if the worst thing in the world had happened to me, only I couldn't for my life have told you the cause. For part of my six-month descent into the darkness, I replayed similar scenes with terrifying frequency, sometimes for days in a row, sometimes more than once a day, literally to the verge of convulsing. And I never knew why—only that I had certain susceptibilities which, when triggered, could lead me to a place of despair so destitute that it made the surface of the moon look inviting. The rest of me looked on, incredulous, waiting for the tide to turn.

As if this were not bad enough, it got worse. High school graduation weekend for Juliana arrived in the spring of 2008. My parents came, accompanied by my brother, and I picked them up at the airport. Clue: If someone you think is perfectly normal picks you up at the airport and says to you out of the blue "I shouldn't be driving," the correct response is to a) take the wheel, and b) ask them why, neither of which happened.

My parents took a suite at a hotel with a second bedroom for me. I remember it principally for its bathroom, where I spent a good deal of time curled up on the cool tile floor under the sink, regrouping. There was a mathematical element to the experience: for every X amount of time I spent in the living room with the family, I would excuse myself and spend Y amount of time under the sink. Then I would get back up and re-join the group, deftly inserting myself into the conversation as if nothing had happened.

It was like the descriptions you hear of people almost freezing to death, where they just want to give up and go to sleep, but that last little spark keeps them moving. One of those times at the hotel when my last little spark kicked in, and I did get up, I went back into the living room and joined everybody at the breakfast table. The waffle I had ordered was at my place, and the scent of the food was overwhelming, because I was so hungry by then; I had eaten so little for months. I ate two bites ravenously and simultaneously had the thought that this was good (healthy recognition of the need for nutrition) and that this was bad (my inner food addict telling me that it was better to starve and stay thin). After two bites I put my fork down, sick to my stomach.

I went early to reserve seats for all of us at the graduation. There was a line, and I took my place at the back, but after a minute I found that I couldn't stand up. I left the line and sat down on a stone bench nearby. I wasn't doing well: I was losing the battle and maybe the war and I knew it. A woman I knew sat down next to me and asked me how I was. What do you tell a person under such circumstances? What should I have been telling anybody? What is our responsibility for each other? For a stranger? A friend? A sister? A daughter? A mother?

Speaking of daughters, I notice that while I am describing Juliana's graduation, it is all about me, not about her as one would hope on such a special day. More than one person had leveled the accusation of selfishness at me, and it is a reasonable one. How do I defend myself against that truth? I have often been absorbed in my struggle, as a fox is absorbed in its effort to chew its leg off in order to escape from a trap.

Graduation was in May 2008, the zenith or the nadir, whichever way you choose to look at it, of my journey through Hell. There were definite religious overtones to the place in which I found myself, dislocating for one who then had so few religious reference points. There was something elemental about watching my mind come apart before my very eyes; the intensity and trance-like nature of the experience reminded me of stories I had read about ascetics in remote caves, although it was my understanding that they achieved divine revelation, while I merely achieved insanity. Perhaps I am mistaken and it is one and the same.

At some point during Juliana's graduation proceedings, I told my brother that I needed help, and he convinced my parents to pay for a treatment program at Farraday, a nationally recognized, private pay facility on the East Coast. I was very lucky to have that option, because according to my doctor at the time, the choices were either top of the line rehab or government facilities that shoved a few pills down your throat and kicked you back onto the street in less than a week.

I landed at the airport in the small town in which Farraday was located and took a taxi to the hospital on a hot day in June of 2008. To this day I fail to understand why people persisted in thinking that it was okay for me to undertake the trip on my own, as if I were taking off on one of my earlier carefree jaunts to Europe, when they all knew that I was in a state of collapse. I'm lucky I didn't end up in Peoria.

I arrived at noon and was shown to a well-appointed office. I assumed that I would be checking in, unpacking, and getting introduced to the program. When the staff started to open my suitcase in the office, I thought, "Well, that's nice that they want to unpack for me, but wouldn't it be more convenient if they did it in my room? Only Suzy Marmalade could have taken this as a hospitality service rather than the drugs and weapons search that it clearly was.

For a long time, I didn't remember much about my hospitalization at Farraday. I knew that I had cried incessantly for the first three weeks. I couldn't get any traction, which made me feel even more desperate. Any improvement seemed to be met with equal or greater regression. I had short-circuited to the point that opening an email brought on a fight or flight response. Bit by bit, the pros at Farraday brought me back from the edge.

Having a community of bright fellow patients from similar backgrounds, sharing similar struggles and equally dedicated to their own recovery helped, as did the perpetual poker games.

Poker was fun at Farraday because we had a couple of players who were perfect foils, an absolutely gorgeous, bronzed West Coast kid who was forever going all in and losing, and a weathered Tennessee stockbroker, Johnson, old enough to be the kid's father, who could read the kid like a book and would goad him into raising and raising when he had absolutely nothing. Johnson won nine times out of ten. Since gambling was not permitted, we bet with artificial sugar packets: pink (Sweet'N Low) was worth $1.00, blue (Equal) $5.00 and yellow (Splenda) $10.00. I confounded everyone at the table because no one believed that anyone could be as inept at bluffing as I was, so they would bet against me and lose every time.

I laughed a lot at that poker table, even when the joke was on me, and I had not laughed like that for a very long time. The games were a welcome distraction from the sense of catastrophe that pervaded my days, and when I was playing I felt more like my old self—not so serious and even lighthearted at times. I benefited tremendously from the social contact and community at Farraday, and I believe that those elements were a large part of the healing that took place there and at the other two hospitals where I was a patient.

One typically Suzy thing that happened during my time at Farraday was that I left in the middle to go pick up my daughter, Rachel, then eleven years old, at camp in upstate New York. If that wasn't mind-bending, I don't know what was— one minute in the hospital, a few hours later pretending to enjoy swaying to "Kumbaya" with the other parents as we watched our children perform skits. I wouldn't have enjoyed that on the best day I ever had, and this was not that day. It was important to me, though, to make that trip to pick up Rachel, maybe to prove to myself and to her that I was still her mother, and I muddled through fairly well for the two days of meeting and greeting, the performances and the packing— right up until we got to the airport from which we were to go our separate ways. Rachel did not know that I couldn't go home with her, and when I told her, she took it badly. I am sure that she had been hoping that I was better and would be coming home and life would go on as usual. I will never forget the moment of our separation in the airport, literally being dragged apart by the friends who thankfully took charge of Rachel and soothed her as I left for the hospital. Getting out of the taxi to re-enter the hospital felt both like a betrayal of Rachel and a replay of that first visit to the eating disorders institute, where I had walked out of the light and into the locked unit. I was more than a little reluctant to re-enter that world.

But I was glad to be back at Farraday and I needed to be back; even my body told me so, in an unusual way. Soon after my return from the trip to pick up Rachel, I lost the ability to write. I had already lost the ability to read anything for pleasure; the only time I had been able to concentrate for months was at work, so as an avid reader and a person dependent on the written word for making a living, being unable to write felt like the final nail in my coffin.

It came on suddenly and strongly: thirty seconds after I would put pen to paper, I would be overcome by nausea and have to run to my room and lie down before I threw up. The doctors were practically dancing in their excitement to see first hand what they diagnosed as a rarely seen condition called a "conversion reaction," an inexplicable physical symptom stemming from anxiety. I was both terrified for myself and outraged at their excitement. It was a huge loss for me: words had been my friends from the very beginning, plus as a lawyer, if I couldn't write, I didn't see how I could work. In any event, given the medication I had been taking, hitting middle age and reaching menopause, my memory had been shot for years and I had the habit of writing everything down as a backstop against forgetfulness. What was I going to do now?

The problem persisted for a long time, even after I left Farraday and went back to work. The nausea went away, but for at least another year I had trouble forming letters, and after I took handwritten notes I had to type them up as fast as I could because they were close to illegible. It was a very humbling experience to have something as basic as my ability to write impaired. Prior to that time I had never had a scintilla of patience, but I remember talking myself through the motions of forming letters quite compassionately.

The only upside I could see was that if I was going to have to go through this kind of shit, it was a welcome thing to have some personal growth to show for it.

CHAPTER FOUR

SUZY MARMALADE GOES
INPATIENT (AGAIN)

I GOT A GREAT DEAL OF HELP at Farraday but apparently not enough, and the next crash came fast. If I were taken down for no other reason, this alone would have been enough: I left Rachel in Virginia with her father in the spring of 2009, moving back to Atlanta where I had "people" in a bid to put my life back together and to help me climb up out of the mire. Rachel visited me that summer, twelve going on pick-a-number, but still twelve after all. She worked as a counselor in training at a summer camp and won the "Calf of the Week" award one week, as opposed to the "Counselor of the Week" or "COW" for the full counselors. She was really pleased and even proud. This was the kind of thing I got to glimpse during the summer weeks when she was with me. She was still willing to hold my hand once in a while as we crossed a street, or even occasionally for no reason at all. There are no words for the pain of absenting myself from her, but I knew when I was working from self-preservation, and this was such a time.

I had a friend, and she really was a friend, with the best of intentions (okay, call me Suzy), who took me to lunch a few months after Rachel left at the end of that summer. She wanted to see how I was doing, aware that I was not in wonderful shape. Midway through lunch, she leaned towards me and said, "You must feel like such a failure." I show shock as mild puzzlement, which she must have seen on my face and felt compelled to explain: "Well, I know I would. You are missing Rachel's growing up, you are not there to help her get ready for parties and watch her get dressed and put on her makeup and see her go off with her friends and...." I didn't hear any more; I had fallen into a time-lapse emotional state and was trying to telescope my feelings enough to come up with a response on the spot. I couldn't do it, so I settled for keeping quiet and waiting until I could go home and inspect my wounds.

There is pain and then there is pain.

My father had died that fall, I was out of a job and I had moved my home too many times (four times in five years). I missed all of my children, not just Rachel. My sense of dislocation was both literal and figurative, and felt altogether final and beyond repair. I knew I was in serious trouble when many of the symptoms I had felt prior to entering Farraday came back. I was teetering on the edge and it frightened me so much that I decided to admit myself as an inpatient again. I checked myself into a local facility, Alexander Hospital, of which I knew nothing but which my psychiatrist at the time, Dr. Renway, recommended to me. As it turned out, she had really thrown me under the bus, into a place that was populated largely by crack addicts and criminals, many of them downright scary. In her defense, Dr. Renway sent me to Alexander because she knew one of the physicians on staff and requested that he oversee my case personally. She just didn't come close to accurately gauging the effect that the environment and patient population would have on me.

Most of the inmates (and I do not use the term loosely) had been in before, knew the ropes, and were expected by the staff to be very creative about ways to get things done, like getting drugs and/or killing themselves. I figured I was an old hand at the suitcase check, no problem. Not true. This time, on check-in the staff didn't just search my suitcase;

they took it away entirely. In return I received two paper grocery bags to hold three days of clothes and toiletries. They took away my cell phone, credit cards, and all cash except $10. Everything else was locked up until checkout. Then I went down to the unit and turned in my shampoo, bar of soap, perfume, makeup, blow dryer and dental floss, to be made available each day only between 7:20 a.m. and 8:00 a.m. The only toiletries I could keep were toothpaste and deodorant.

So out of necessity I became a thief for the first time in my life (not technically true: I shoplifted M&Ms a couple of times in college, the pound bag). On the third morning, I palmed six or seven of my dental floss strings and hid them in my underwear. My mornings were looking up.

I didn't bring either, but others had to turn in belts and shoe laces. This one poor kid had come in wearing really baggy pants *à la* "Look Like a Fool With Your Pants on the Ground" of *American Idol* fame. Once they took his belt, at any given moment his pants were for real either on the ground or on their way down.

The lights were fluorescent and the voices loud at Alexander. It was nothing like the comfortable hotel-like feeling of Farraday, where the ceilings were high and the rooms spacious and lit softly with table lamps, single occupancy with private bathrooms. I don't think I saw one lamp inside the living space at Alexander. Presumably the glass light bulbs were too risky. The rooms were small, with beds that were more like cots than real beds. There were two people to a room, sharing one small bathroom and a tiny closet space, which didn't matter since each of us had only the items in our grocery bags. There were no rugs, just linoleum; in a word, institutional. If you weren't already depressed, your surroundings were guaranteed to put you right over the edge.

It is not possible to overstate the social displacement that I felt once I got the measure of my surroundings at Alexander. Forget what it looked like, I was on a hall with crack addicts who had tracks in places I'd never heard of, alcoholics going through the D.T.s, fresh suicide attempts displaying bright red stitches, severe sexual abuse survivors, people with teeth missing, people with no teeth, criminals and people who were just plain raving mad—psychotic, delusional, schizophrenic or a combination. It was a modern-day equivalent of Bedlam: not the best choice for my recovery but a perfect pick if you wanted to skip the acid and go on the trip anyway.

To say that this was a shock to my system, to everything that had gone into the making of me up to that point, is putting it mildly. By any objective standard, I had been extraordinarily sheltered and inordinately spoiled, and between the two, I was ill prepared for this kind of collision of worlds.

This was apparent from the very first night. A group of us was playing Spades and the question of our transportation to the hospital came up. Two people had come strapped to gurneys with arm restraints. One had been dropped off by his wife. That was Roger, a young country boy who had been unable to sleep for many nights in a row in reaction to medication, which kicked in his depression. The night his wife brought him to the hospital, he was in the bathroom with his shotgun up under his chin, cocked and about to pull the trigger. I mentioned that I had driven myself in. With newfound respect, Roger said: "You're not as dumb as I thought you were." (He's the cracker, I'm the lawyer.) Apparently I was being given points for planning my escape in advance. Too bad I had to tell him that I had only driven my own car because that's what my doctor told me to do.

As I settled into the program at Alexander, I began to find some humor in the goings on, so different from what I had experienced at Farraday. Take the staff, for example. One day during my week as a full-time locked up patient at the hospital, we had an unusual group session. Typically, the topics were positive thinking, spirituality, self- esteem, relapse prevention and the like. I had to give the staff people credit. They worked for a facility that did not pay well (we knew this because they were forever on their cell phones setting up job interviews) and were stretched as thin as fishing wire, yet they did a great job, usually professional and intent on engaging the group.

Except this time. Gloria, a young social worker, took the floor and from the get go she let it rip. Her topic was not readily apparent, but after paying close attention I figured out that it was about how Gloria's boyfriend had gone out with her friend behind her back and what Gloria had done about it. Gloria seemed pretty pissed, and I wondered how she had found the fortitude to access her coping skills. What did she try? Deep breathing? No. Journaling? No. Reaching out to a friend? No. Talking through it with her friend and boyfriend? No. Praying about it? No. None of the above.

We got treated to a bravura performance of *Medea Goes Medieval on Yo Ass*. It was a butt-twitching, finger shaking, hour-long rant that flew in the face of everything in my carefully annotated, heavily highlighted recovery notebook. It was hysterically funny, some of the best theater I have ever seen. "He think he gonna play me the fool??? I don't think so!!! I'm gonna take his sorry ass and carry it over to his cousin's house and beat the crap out of him. I'm gonna..." and on and on. Interspersed with her ravings she made some notations on the blackboard that we were to jot down. I think they had to do with setting boundaries.

It occurred to me that sometimes being an inpatient at Alexander was like wandering through the pages of *A Hitchhiker's Guide to the Galaxy*, but without the guide. This notion was reinforced a few days later when I was talking to Bernice, another of the staff people, one whom I had gotten to know a little bit. She was an older white lady with gray hair, a little roly poly and generally nicer than the rest, more willing to make sure you got your phone calls and to hand out the toiletries early enough so that you didn't miss breakfast. I was shooting the breeze with Bernice, leaning up against the Plexiglass that separated us from S Section, home to the psychotic, violent patients. I commented that she must have seen and heard some really crazy things in her days working at a psychiatric hospital, particularly if she had been stationed on S Section. She agreed, but on reflection noted that she had only had one patient who said he was abducted by aliens. She continued: "But I've seen lights in the sky that weren't normal."

I dug into my memories from younger days when I read a lot of science fiction: "Do you think they were meteors?" "No." Digging deeper while retaining the fond hope that this was going to be a sane conversation in spite of the direction it seemed to be taking, I said, "Do you think they were from the government?" "No," said Bernice, "I think they were a metal and organic hybrid created in a tank and brought here from the future to observe us."

This was not a joke. I could tell from her expression that the woman was 100% serious. I retreated to my room to consider how I could possibly have thought of killing myself when life was so endlessly entertaining.

CHAPTER FIVE

SUICIDE BY BLENDER

WHEN I SAY THAT I had thought of killing myself before I checked into Alexander, it was not something that I had ever planned actively. I had no stash of pills, no drugs, no gun, nothing like that. I was more passive—life seemed too painful, and if something were to happen to me, maybe that would have been all right, but I never got to the point of helping it along.

The best example I remember is being asleep one morning and waking up a little to feel my cat, Horace, raking at my arm with his claws. That wasn't unusual, there were many mornings when he would pull his claws through my hair to wake me so he could get fed, such a funny feeling, like having my hair combed by the cat. Sometimes, it was playful, sometimes not so, and when he was really hungry, he would get mad and exert enough pressure to hurt. This particular morning he must have been starving, because all of a sudden I felt him dig a claw into my arm and push. It hurt a lot, and being half awake, instead of working my arm loose, I pulled it away fast. I felt a long and deep tear, the kind of sensation that would have caused anyone else to leap up and check whether they had blood pouring down their arm and needed to go to the hospital. Not me, not in the state that I was in. I lay there and considered that I might be badly hurt, that Horace might have hit a vein or an artery and I might be losing a lot of blood, or at the very least risking a bad infection if I didn't clean it out. Then I lay there some more. I didn't move, didn't even roll over. I just lay there and did nothing. I wondered about it a little, in a detached sort of way, but not enough to look at my arm, which was still flung over the side of the bed as it had been when Horace clawed me. I stayed that way for a very long time, until I finally decided that I really had to get up and go to work. I sat up and glanced down at my arm. Sure enough, there was about a three inch gash, all the way along the top of my forearm, but I had been lucky—it was deep but more of a slice than a serious wound. There was some blood dripping down, but not enough to require a visit to the hospital, and it looked like it would heal okay without stitches. I didn't care enough to find out, so I took a shower, got dressed and went to work.

Most people have no idea what it feels like to be so down that life's end would seem a blessing. I have described the emotional and spiritual distress that accompanied the decline leading to my admission to Farraday, and many of the same symptoms dogged me as I checked into Alexander. About two weeks into the program at Alexander, it occurred to me that it might be useful to give the hospital psychiatrist a list of those daily physical symptoms to help with my treatment. In less than three minutes I jotted down on the back of an envelope what came immediately to mind: trouble drawing a deep breath, shoulders hunched and tight, bones popping in my neck, twitching, aching jaw from clenching my teeth (I later found out that I was grinding my teeth so hard in my sleep that I had inflamed the roots), trouble falling asleep, waking up three to four times a night, hot and cold, shaking violently, particularly in the hours after waking up, blurred and grainy vision, chattering teeth, trouble writing by hand, constantly losing my balance, often getting extremely fatigued while driving, tightness in my chest, feeling like my blood was sizzling, sudden high blood pressure, inability to concentrate, emotionally and mentally paralyzed (completely unable to make a decision or take an action), panicked, racing thoughts from the minute I woke up 'til the minute I fell asleep, feelings of extreme despair, disoriented, some self-harm thoughts, severe memory loss, losing access to words and spelling, being extremely irritable, no longer driving automatically but having to think myself through it every time I turned the wheel, braked, or speeded up, and lyrics from songs looping around and around and around in my head.

These were merely the symptoms that popped into my head without having to think about it, so an end to all of that didn't seem too unpalatable. It's a fine line, though, between passive thoughts of suicide and the act itself, and just how fine was brought home to me when I returned to my apartment from my week locked inside Alexander.

Often a full-time inpatient is moved over to the outpatient program for more rehab before full release, and that's what I did, coming in several days a week but going home after. A couple of days after the switch, I went to make my morning protein shake and couldn't find my mini-blender. I looked in some pretty routine places first: the dishwasher, all of the kitchen cabinets, under the kitchen sink. Then I branched out: the refrigerator, freezer, kitchen drawers, under the bathroom sink, other places I kept supplies. Then I reflected on the fact that I had just been in a psychiatric hospital and maybe my wires had been a little crossed. So I tried the coat closet, the linen closet, the bookshelf, my dresser drawers and the balcony. I finally gave up and forgot about it for a while.

Later, I called my cousin, Erin, to chat. The blender popped into my head and I told her the story. She said, "Did you look in the bag?" I said, "What bag?" "The bag with all of the stuff that we took out of your house."

During my family conference on the fifth day I was inpatient, Erin told me that the day after I was admitted, the hospital had called my family and asked them to go to my apartment and take out everything I could use to try to kill myself. My cousin lived nearest, so she went with her daughter-in-law and gathered everything up. She later told me that she went around first and then her savvier daughter-in-law went behind and found twice as much again. I never asked whether the mini-blender made round one or round two. I decided round two, had to be, but I appreciated the vote of confidence in my creativity.

CHAPTER SIX

LIFE IN THE 'HOOD

I LEARNED A LOT OF LESSONS about life in the "'hood" inside the hospital walls, particularly in the cafeteria. One of our group at Alexander was a young man, twenty-two years old, half Hispanic and half Asian, very street smart. He was adorable, irrepressible, a complete mess with an impish smile and equally impish ways. Three of the women, including me, took him on to raise, and he could and did get away with anything he wanted to.

I often noticed his m.o. in the cafeteria, which was a scene unlike any other: bright lights, bursts of shouting, people wandering around aimlessly, staff bellowing for people to get back where they belonged, patients trying to score (cigarettes, mainly). There we all were, every day, and this kid would mess around there just like everywhere else. He would fool around with people's food, plates, trays. Everybody would bring him second desserts, extra food, most anything he wanted. He always asked with a broad smile and received with a broader one, lips curling up in the corners.

One day, the kid started messing with an older black woman, Angela. He was sitting on my right, she was across from him, and next to her was one of the other "mothers," a light-skinned black woman in the military. I was minding my own business, and the next thing I knew the kid and Angela were on their feet screaming back and forth at each other: "I am gonna cut your mother-fucking dick off and shove it down your throat! I'm gonna take your cock-sucking dick and rip it off and kill you!" (In the midst of the uproar I remember noticing that it was a little unusual that they were both screaming about cutting each other dicks off even though one of them was ostensibly a woman.) Angela picked up a fork and started jabbing it at the kid's face. He was about to come over the table and do God knows what to her. The staff didn't mobilize, but I was panicked and everyone else at the table looked pretty concerned. Mom #2 got up and intervened military-style, dragging Angela away, fork and all. She got Angela settled down, but for a few final lunges and muttered curses, and the kid finally backed off as well.

It turned out that he had drummed his silverware on the table and then bounced his tray lightly on top of hers. That's all it took to set Angela off. It didn't seem like much to me and the fork seemed like a big overreaction, but the consensus, among old folks and young punk gang members alike, was that the kid was in the wrong. I don't mean a few people, I mean every single member of the younger generation of African American alcoholic/junkie/ low-income/boyz in the 'hood/girlz in the club/ teenage mother/gang member/criminal/eighth-grade-education patients. According to them, "Miss Angela" was his elder and deserved respect, plain and simple. He shouldn't have messed with her tray and he never ever should have raised his voice to her or said nasty things, no matter what she said or did to him. I felt chastised to hear such respect from a part of our culture that I had been taught had no respect other than for celebrities, gang leaders and rappers.

During the post-mortem, Mom #2 commented that she and I would never have let anything happen to Angela; we would have jumped the kid and beaten the crap out of him if it came to that. I'm glad it didn't, since I would have hated to have disappointed anybody. Everybody agreed that if the kid didn't quit "playing," he would be dead or in jail by the time he was thirty.

How to stop a fork fight wasn't the only street lesson I learned in the cafeteria at Alexander. One day, I stood behind a new patient in the lunch line. He had multiple street names but told me that I could call him Halo. Word was that at the ripe age of twenty-five, he was a big time crack addict who had driven the getaway car in a botched attempted theft of drug money from some local dealers in a big Midwestern city. I felt somewhat nostalgic when I heard the part about wrapping his father's immaculate Lincoln Continental around a tree, because it reminded me of the time in high school when I almost drove my brother's beloved 442 into a river. (Bored with studying for exams one winter day, I had taken his car for a spin on a muddy track near the local Chattahoochee River and slid off the track sideways, all the way down the ice-covered hill towards the river, coming to a stop about ten yards from its banks. I caught hell for that one, since it took three wreckers and two weeks to drag the car back up the hill.) I had no other reaction to Halo's story, since by this time someone's criminal background was ho-hum news to me, one more friend from the underworld.

I followed Halo to the iced tea dispenser and watched him fill a foam cup or two, then put twenty-five or thirty sugar packets on the tray next to his lunch plate. I made a quick judgment that he was a wasteful person and didn't mind throwing away someone else's money if it gave him something to play with. As with many things at Alexander, my judgment was based on a completely irrelevant frame of reference and therefore missed the mark by a country mile.

I sat down near Halo and ate my usual sandwich. After a while, my ears picked up a foreign sound, repetitious and annoying. I looked around and saw that it was Halo with his sugar— rip, pour, rip, pour—18, 19, 20, 21 times. What the hell? I mean, I had eaten white bread, butter, and sugar sandwiches at summer camp when there was nothing else to snack on (that was in the 1960s and white bread was still acceptable), but twenty-five packets of sugar at a sitting? Then I noticed the look on his face and the set of his shoulders, tense and hunched, and I knew that something wasn't right. I asked the woman next to me what was going on, and she told me that when you are withdrawing from crack and you've got nothing else to take the edge off, large quantities of sugar will help. I meant to ask Halo if he knew that or just ate the sugar because he craved it, but he was sent to another program (detox?) before I got the chance.

Halo may have had his sugar packets, but everyone else at Alexander had his or her cigarettes, and there was a whole subculture that existed around smoking. I know from experience that the one thing they will not take away from a patient at a mental institution is cigarettes. From the upscale patients at Farraday, the fancy East Coast hospital I'd gone to in 2008, to the low-income addicts at Alexander, all smokers got to keep their cigarettes and the staff were unusually compliant about opening the door on time for them to go outside and smoke. A doctor had explained to me that by the time people reached the doorstep of a mental institution, they needed to be put back together, not taken further apart, so the quit-smoking campaigns were off limits for the time being.

I hated it. These institutions have limited green space, usually an enclosed courtyard of dirt and dead grass, and when that space is filled with dense clouds of cigarette smoke, it's hard for non-smokers like me to get a breath of fresh air. At Alexander I remember gathering my coat against the cold (it was February), taking a deep breath, holding it, and racing past the newly lit up smokers to the other end of the little courtyard to gulp a breath or two of untainted air before the smoke wafted down that way. Almost everybody besides me, white, black, young, old, country, city, male or female, smoked. I watched people come and go, having for reasons best known to God the longest running insurance authorization at Alexander on record, and the percentage of non-smokers was close to zero.

No one loathes cigarettes more than an ex-smoker. As a smoker, I was in the blue ribbon category, smoking upwards of two packs of Marlboros a day. I tried to cut down by using those sissy filters they introduced in the 1970s. This was during law school, and my fellow students thought me unbearably affected, but the filters were purely functional, supposedly trapping the tar and nicotine. You had to clean them out after every couple of cigarettes with a little twisted up Kleenex. I visited a friend in Chicago at the height of this period and long after I was gone she kept finding filthy black strips of tissue in unlikely places, all clotted with tar. I don't remember being such a slob, but I guess I was. So was she, so that was okay. The sad part about the filters was that the more I used them, the more I smoked, so by the time I decided that they were useless, I was up to almost three packs a day. (I once observed my cat having the same experience with his diet cat food, working on me for four meals a day rather than two.)

I quit smoking in 1984 on a whim, and it couldn't have been more painless. My accidental and wildly successful technique was that I never intended to quit, I just accepted a bet that I would go a single day without smoking. I went that day and then another and another, and with some well-timed, completely unsolicited encouragement from my friends ("You can do it!"... "Do what?"), after three weeks I was done with cigarettes. I have only smoked twice since, both times unintentionally. The first time was a peace pipe, which was completely disgusting. God knows what they used as tobacco. (This was incidental to the "Suzy Marmalade tries Native American culture to heal herself" campaign.) The second time was in Amsterdam. I went into a coffee shop and asked for a joint, and when they asked me what kind, I said, "I don't know, something mild." Even in college I had never smoked a joint by myself, so I was wondering halfway through why I wasn't more stoned. My friend at the bar took a hit and explained that it was half cigarette tobacco, which is what they give you in Amsterdam when you ask for something mild. I will say that although it tasted horrible it was pretty mellow.

At Alexander, it was strange to watch everyone else buy, sell and barter cigarettes (25 cents each). It was reminiscent of everything I'd read about prisons: bribing the guards with cigarettes, using them as currency with the other inmates. Watching my fellows fiddle with their cigarettes and glance up at the clock, waiting for the staff to announce smoke break, then race to the door and line up to shuffle past the orderly one by one, to lean over while he flicked his lighter for them (patients weren't allowed to carry their own matches or lighters), put me in a mind of a chain gang. Prisons and chain gangs were on the top of the list of places I had not expected to visit in my lifetime.

My street lessons continued after I graduated to the outpatient program at Alexander. On Mondays, I would get filled in on the big stories of the preceding weekend. One Monday, I came in and heard that Mr. M had shared a huge story in the 8:00 a.m. group session. Mr. M was a great friend and sometimes Spades partner of mine from inpatient days. He had graduated as well, but was living on campus in the off hours.

It seems that on the previous Friday evening he had slid down into a very low place and mentally lost the struggle for his sobriety from crack. He walked off campus and down the street to his drug dealer's house.

When I heard this part, much as I was feeling for my friend, I thought, "Wait a minute, are you telling me that you can actually *walk* to a drug dealer's house from the hospital that I am counting on for my recovery?" Apparently, yes.

Mr. M got to the drug dealer's house and the dealer not only refused to sell him drugs, but took him by the arm, walked him back to the border of the hospital campus and sent him across, drug-free. I have a friend who was an Assistant U.S. Attorney for twenty-five years and practiced criminal defense work before that. She said that of all the stories I told her about my stay in the hospital, this was the one that surprised her the most.

Another time during my outpatient stay, I took a trip to the real "'hood." I had been hanging out and chatting with a couple of women friends. One was a very bright young doctor, a yuppie type, heavy into Christianity. She was constantly networking, making sure that anyone and everyone who could help another out was in the loop. After a while, she got up to leave and so did a down-and-out guy to whom she was apparently giving a ride somewhere. I knew him from several weeks in the program; he seemed to be a very sweet-natured guy, in his forties, would give you the shirt off his back. They went out together, then after a couple of minutes, he came back in alone. "What's the matter, Richard," I said, "you lose your ride?" "Yeah." Without giving it any thought, I said, "Where you going? I can give you a ride." "Downtown."

My car was in the shop and I had borrowed my mother's. My mother lived an upscale life, owned two cars, both Lexuses, one an SUV, and one a two-seater coupe. We had had a conversation that morning about which car I should take and decided on the SUV, considering that the hospital was very much on the other side of the tracks.

As we walked up to the car, I said to Richard "Where downtown?" "I have to go see my probation officer; it's off of Green Street." Hmmm. "But I have to make a stop first." Oh. "I have to stop by my apartment and get some papers." Shit. As I saw it, I had two problems: one, my safety, and two, the preservation of my mother's car. Following Richard's directions to his apartment, we pulled up at a deserted complex of worn two-story apartments and he went in. I looked around and hit the lock button. I had gone with Lester, my mother's right hand man, to his apartment in the projects when

I was in my teens, and from time to time as a child I had visited with my Thursday night babysitter at her broken down house in a bad section of town. I had even dated a guy whose house was in such an awful neighborhood that when I spent the night, I stayed up all night peering through his bedroom window shades at my father's pale yellow Cadillac Seville, sure that it was never going to make it out of there in one piece.

So it wasn't like I had never been to the 'hood before, just that I had never been there ALONE but for the company of a strange man of whom I knew nothing except that he was a drug addict, albeit by all appearances a nice one. The clock kept ticking, and my mind moved into darker and darker places. I was alone in my car in a bad neighborhood in an empty apartment complex that looked a lot like places I saw discussed on the evening news, and not in a good way. There was nothing moving, not even the branches of the dead trees scattered around the courtyard, and I started thinking about who might be lurking behind all of those closed doors, and how many knives and guns might be in there with them, and what they might do if they came out and saw me, sitting behind the wheel of my fancy car. For once (never to be repeated), I actually wished that I was still inpatient at Alexander, so I'd be wearing the same dirty jogging suit for the fourth day in a row, my hair hanging limp and my jewelry hidden in a sock, instead of dressed and coiffed in style, with rings sparkling on both hands.

When Richard finally came out with his papers, I felt a sense of relief akin to salvation; and while it was an unorthodox cure for depression, all I can say is that at that moment I was as happy as a clam. To Richard I acted nonchalant, as if this was all in a day's work for me, and we got on the highway. So far, so good. With some trepidation but feeling very streetwise, I asked Richard what he had been in for. "They got me with a pound bag of marijuana in the front seat." Okay, not so bad. As he kept talking, I got the feeling that there was more to it (references to "being in my addiction"), but I didn't ask.

We finally got to the facility (there was no name on the building or sign in front, which I thought was strange). I dropped Richard off, said a prayer that things would go well with his "attitudinous" probation officer, as Richard called him, and got that SUV the hell home.

CHAPTER SEVEN

GROUP UNITY

THERE WERE MANY DIFFERENT KINDS of people in the group at Alexander: all different races, well-to-do, poor (more common), alcoholic, crack addict, pain killer addict, depressed, anxious, psychotic, delusional, old, young, Bible thumper (almost everybody) and spiritual traveler (by our admission, me and two other people). Most of us shared our desire to get better, move on and enjoy life, but little else. Occasionally, though, there were moments when we all thought with one mind and felt with one heart. These were the result of some real show stoppers (rare in a mental institution, since every day usually had its share of outer galactic experiences), when everybody collectively stopped in his or her tracks and forgot to breathe.

In early April, we heard a first step (part of the Alcoholics Anonymous model of recovery) from a comfy cozy middle-aged white woman, placid-seeming. Part of a first step is to describe the two best and two worst experiences of your life. It seems that in her youth, Ellen was Miss Popularity. In twelfth grade, she was voted prom queen. When I squinted I could almost see it, mostly in her smile and in her eyes, and I could imagine her long red hair swept up high. One of the high points of her life was the feeling when they announced her name and she was in her beautiful dress and everybody started clapping and yelling. I think she described riding around on a float, but I was half asleep at that point. Everybody sighed, thinking, "Well, this is going to be a load of crap, hope it's over soon." The second high point was when Ellen had a son, and that seemed natural enough— almost all of the mothers counted their children as high points. She went on about that for a while, too. "John was the sweetest little boy, had all this blonde hair, fixed his own cereal when he was two, dressed up as a lollipop for Halloween." She had a really sweet Southern accent and the word "two" had about three syllables.

Then Ellen recounted, with emotion but not melodrama, her two worst experiences. They were bad, awful, and to hear them from this pink-cheeked, slightly rotund former prom queen took our collective breath away. She first explained that at age nineteen she had been raped. Maybe most of us hadn't heard rape described in person in detail before. Certainly not with such dignity. Then Ellen described her other worst experience, which I cannot write down on paper, that's how bad it was, literally unbearable to hear. Ellen gave us all something to think about: if a sweet, giddy little lady could survive this magnitude of trouble and talk about it without sounding like she was eating glass, what did that say about our complaints?

A few days later, Tommy joined the outpatient program at Alexander. Right after he walked into the small, windowless room where morning check-in group was held, we started going around our group saying how we were feeling and our goal for the day. Tommy was a nice looking, well-built, middle-aged black man, but at first glance you wouldn't say he was physically intimidating. Then, out of the blue, he cut someone off in mid-sentence and words started pouring out of him, not yelling but clipped to the point of being robotic.

I have read phrases in books like "palpable rage," but I have never experienced it, and I have lived with people who did rage to a "T." Frustration, pain, anger, anguish and aggression rocketed around the room. He was a father, divorced, out of work, and his ex-wife was dragging him to court every other week. I remember him repeating over and over, "I'm a good father, I'm not one of those deadbeat dads. I do everything I can to take care of my kids, but I can't get a job. I love my wife, but she says all I do is argue with her. I'm afraid that if I see my ex-wife, I'll hurt her." I believed that he would. I wasn't sure he wasn't going to hurt me right then and there just for looking at him. We all sat there, barely breathing.

And then there was the real show-stopper. One day in outpatient therapy we were having a session on anger. The staff person leading the session put a question to the group: "How do other people know when you are angry?" (At the base of many addictions and depressive disorders is repressed anger, capable of being registered or expressed only with great difficulty.) A female voice came out of the back: "Because I'm a stone killer...."

I had seen *The Professional*, and I had a clear idea in my mind of what type of person a stone killer is—someone like Leon, the main character in the movie, who kills with no remorse, no regret, pitiless, usually for money, a hit man. I was in the front of the room, and as I slowly swiveled to look at Mary, I watched every head in the room, regardless of race, creed, or color, turn with me. Then, as if choreographed, we turned and looked at each other. I said to the young crack addict next to me, "Did I just hear what I thought I just heard?" "Uh huh," he said. We all shook our heads, speechless.

Mary was an Appalachian-looking woman, tall and on the husky side, with short, stringy hair. I hadn't heard her say much, only that she had a twelve-year-old daughter back home whom she was afraid to visit because her abusive ex-husband might come by. What kind of a person inspires fear in a self-described stone killer?

I only had that kind of experience of group unity one other time in my life, and the circumstances were so different that it made me wonder about time and space and the connection of seemingly random events. I was riding a bus in Hong Kong, one that I took frequently; it must have been 1995 or 1996. The bus ran from the Wan Chai district to the South Side of Hong Kong Island, and I would exit at Stanley, others at Repulse Bay or points between. There were many different groups on the bus, and we all tolerated each other, but no more than that.

The Chinese men drove everybody crazy screaming "Wei???!!!" ("Hello!") into their cell phones and launching into interminable phone calls conducted at the top of their lungs. The Filipina maids annoyed everyone with their Amah bags (large, square, red, white, and blue plaid plastic bags) stuffed to the gills with beauty products and other paraphernalia, squeezed next to them on their seats, on the floor, in the overhead racks, or anywhere one could be jammed. The British contributed stuffiness that seeped from every pore. The Aussies were irritating for their ridiculous exuberance, like small children let out for recess, only most of them were anything but small.

We Americans were an insult to the brisk commerce of the place, with our slack-jawed faces and cow-like demeanors. I have always thought that our language promotes this: there is no force to the way we expel our words, as opposed to the Europeans and Asians I have observed, who blow their cheeks out, purse their lips, squint and grimace with almost every character, giving far greater exercise and thereby far greater definition to their faces. Maybe slack jaws are more strictly a phenomenon in the South, where half- swallowed phrases barely escape with their lives.

Day after day, we all rubbed along, chafing at the heat and biding our time until we reached our stop. This particular day the bus was proceeding at a normal pace, the route the same as the week before and the one before that, and all the preceding months. Suddenly, the driver went off course, took a right turn where we were all used to going straight. For a moment, silence. You could hear everybody's wheels turning in unison: "This isn't the way, why did he turn? I didn't see a roadblock, is there something the driver knows that I don't? I don't want to go this way, I want to go the way we usually go. This might be longer, hotter, slower. I might be late." We all looked at each other, looked at the driver, and in many languages but with one voice said, "You've taken a wrong turn, what are you doing? You should have gone straight back there and instead you turned!" We were outraged, individually and collectively, to a person.

It turned out to be a mistake; we were all right and the driver was wrong. He turned around, no mean feat on those narrow roads, and soon we were back on the correct route, as if nothing had happened.

But something had. I know it, because it made such an impression on me, one that I haven't forgotten in all these years. There was a striking sense of harmony in the air, of unity, not unlike descriptions I have heard of life during power blackouts in New York, only more so. Exactly like the reaction at Alexander after we heard Mary's description of herself as a "stone killer." I have tried many times to break it down, to isolate the essential elements of the bus incident, because I really do believe that there is a lesson to be learned there. We were twenty-five to thirty people, in close quarters, sharing a habitual activity, predisposed to focus on our differences but drawn together this once by an adverse event of vexing, not alarming, proportions. This last part is critical: it can't be a catastrophe because then our minds would have run amuck and the sense of unity lost.

I would like to replicate the event, have an international day when all bus drivers are secretly told to go off route, to see what happens. This is the kind of shit I think about, so perhaps it's a good thing I'm not in charge.

CHAPTER EIGHT

NEWS TO ME

COURTESY OF MY FELLOW patients at Alexander, I learned that:

1. Rabbit tobacco is some kind of natural "weed" that country people smoke. It grows wild in the South.
2. The Bluffs is a small area near the Georgia Dome in Atlanta: the ninth circle of Hell, you can buy anything there—weed, crack, kids—and if you are Suzy Marmalade (i.e., white and lacking street smarts), you are dead on sight.

3. A folk cure for bumps or freckles on your face is to take the tee-tee of a newborn baby, let the diaper get really wet, and hold the wet diaper to your face.
4. "CS" means constant supervision—the really risky people coming into the hospital got a tail like in the spy movies.
5. "PO" means probation officer.
6. There is a country expression, "Fine as frog's hair split 3 ways." I don't know what it means, but it sounds colorful.
7. In Appalachia, "kern" means a terrible odor.
8. There is a TV show called *Dog the Bounty Hunter* and I love it.
9. It is possible to shoot up and drive at the same time. A junkie I met at Alexander told me that his need for a fix got so frequent at one point that sometimes when he was driving the Beltway around D.C., he would steer the car with his knees while he pulled the rubber tube tight around one arm with his teeth and shot up with the other hand. Oprah Winfrey may have done a great job campaigning against texting while driving, but based on this I think she should have expanded her horizons.
10. Ebay means more than you think it does.

I think of myself as the Ebay queen. I love it so much that it is the only stock that I have bought without anybody's advice for ages (a whopping

$500 investment, but that is a testament more to the sorry state of my personal finances at the time than to my faith in Ebay). I used to sell vintage handbags from a booth in an antiques mall in a small Southern town. I sourced 98% of the bags on Ebay, no frustrating days at estate/junk sales for me. I developed lists of search words and techniques that took me way below the radar, so I got great deals. I bought clothes on Ebay (NWT only), electronics (usually got burned, but the prices were irresistible), books, bed linens, theme gifts (my mother loves poodles and my brother had mentioned an interest in beagles, so those were a big focus for a while), tickets to sold-out sports events (or at least used it to compare to Stubhub), and pots and pans for my apartment. I cheated by using ezsniper.com, swooping in at the last minute with my finely tuned bid, very satisfying.

Clearly I had spent an inordinate amount of time on Ebay, and I didn't expect other people to be as familiar with the site as I was. But to overhear a fellow patient at Alexander say matter-of-factly, "I am looking forward to finding my brother on Ebay," well, I had a real impulse to call Meg Whitman (I still thought of her and Ebay as synonymous) and let her know that they had a live one out there.

Postscript: I later discovered a phenomenon that explained why "finding my brother on Ebay" made sense. On my last day at Alexander, we were waiting for the check-in group to start. A guy across the room admired my purse. "I bought it on Ebay." While I answered his questions about how Ebay works I overhead a second guy hold forth about how he had read something from the Book of Revelations on the site the night before and it had really rocked his world. Somebody else chimed in and all of a sudden it clicked: to some people, "Ebay" means the internet like "Kleenex" means tissues. Take that to the bank, Meg.

CHAPTER NINE

SANITY IS RELATIVE

O SECTION (FOR "OPEN"), where I was housed during my inpatient stay at Alexander, was a mixed bag—people with depression and anxiety, drug addicts, alcoholics, people who had attempted suicide, you name it—but it was consistent in that none of our conditions posed a threat against others. S Section (for "Secure"), not O Section, was for the delusional, paranoid, schizophrenic and violent. It abutted our section and sometimes we would hear people yelling and hitting things, even once trying to make a break for it through our section.

We did have one paranoid delusional of our very own in O Section; perhaps S Section had run out of space. Ed was a white guy, older than most of us at about sixty-five years old, probably not bad looking, except that his face usually was contorted or pained or sad, never smooth. He yelled, he screamed, he cried, he muttered, he wore braided towels over his head and more than anything, he preached. It was real Southern Baptist—wonderful cadences, eyes cast unblinkingly toward the ceiling. He went through a phase of being obsessively solicitous at lunch, where he would fetch drinks for us, clean up after us and take all of our trays back when we were done. For a long time I was terrified of him, but when I saw that I seemed to be the only one, I started saying "hi" and then talking to him a little. We were on good terms by the time I left the inpatient program and said a friendly goodbye and good luck.

A couple of weeks after I left O Section for the day program, my doctor ordered a blood test. He asked me to come early the next morning when the lab person would be there to draw blood. I did so, and was led into a locked unit and parked in a chair in a corridor while someone looked for the lab tech. Almost immediately, I noticed something wrong in the air, and it felt so strange and I felt so exposed that I turned my eyes to the floor and kept them there, hoping not to be noticed. Someone pulled at my clothes and I looked up—

an unfamiliar woman wanted to know if I wanted to be prayed over (I said yes), and another woman whirled by in some kind of intricate dance. Then a familiar voice: "What are you doing over here??!" Ed walked up to me and I have never been so happy to see anyone in my life. "I'm not here for good, I'm just waiting to get blood drawn. What are you doing?" "They moved me over to S Section a few days ago."

That explained why my hair was standing on end. The staff had parked me in the corridor in the middle of the paranoid delusional patient population without telling me. I finally got my blood drawn (fruitlessly—I had forgotten to go without breakfast), said my second goodbye to Ed and returned to the other side.

I visited four worlds that day: S Section (total madness), the outpatient program (partial madness), the workaday world that most people live in, and that night, at a dinner party for my mother's eighty-fifth birthday, the world where people discuss where one can have one's grandmother's Belgian lace table linens cleaned for less than $300. The fascinating part was that I could relate to each one.

As topsy-turvy as my world was, I always knew at some level that I was still sane, that I had a functional brain that was not beset by truly faulty wiring or an incurable chemical imbalance. Not even Ed struck me as that far gone, for at least he had periods of lucidity. In all my time at Alexander, I had only one interaction with someone who I thought was truly insane, and it was chilling. Jeffrey walked in one day and sat down with our group for morning check-in. When the staff person got around to him, she asked the same question that she always asked of the rest of us: "What are your goals for today?" Jeffrey: "To work on my listening skills." So far so good: that was a typical answer that a lot of people gave, since it was a skill that was taught and reinforced frequently in our sessions. "And how are you going to do that?" Jeffrey: "I hear voices inside my head and I'm going to listen to them. It could be a lot of voices or it could be a single voice. I'm going to listen to them all." From the look in his eyes I knew that he was gone, just plain gone, and if he was ever to come back, he had a long way to travel. I felt so sorry for him, because I was pretty sure that even with all the willingness in the world and any amount of hard work, he wasn't going to come back; for him there was no choice.

Aside from people with more serious issues like Ed and Jeffrey, most of the people I met at Alexander were closer to where I was on the spectrum of mental and emotional distress, suffering from issues ranging from depression to anxiety to obsessive compulsive disorder and other similar conditions, all generally coupled with an abiding sense of feeling overwhelmed. As a result, despite differences in skin color, age, drug of choice and other details, there was a great deal of mutual understanding and compassion, and the unlikeliest people became friends with each other. (Translation: misery loves company.) Beyond that, occasionally it would turn out that once you got past the apparent differences, there were surprising parallels. The commonalities I found with a woman named "Timmy" were a good example.

Timmy was in her late twenties, a tightly wrapped woman often quivering with anger, but intent on better managing her emotions and her life. She was from a big city, which is always a plus for me, and I had thought for a while that maybe we could be friends as long as I was careful about how much I was exposed to her sometimes toxic level of anger.

I made a few efforts to get to know Timmy, but for the longest time I could not make any headway. Then one day towards the end of my outpatient program at Alexander, Timmy started to open up. We had been asked by the staff person leading the group to say a little about our background. Timmy noted, casually: "I am the daughter of a black Jewish mother and a white father." Oh, interesting, this could be a signal that we were indeed meant to be friends. Maybe I could talk to her about her Jewish background—I had just celebrated Passover this past week with my family. I wasn't aware of any other Jewish patients and certainly not Timmy, a black woman, so this was encouraging—a "landsman," as they called it in the old days in

Europe. (It means "kin" or something to that effect in Yiddish.) My father, despite being the southern, *Driving Miss Daisy* kind of Jewish, had loved his story of unexpectedly encountering a "landsman" selling him a souvenir in some remote part of Italy. Now I had my very own "landsman-appears-out-of-the-blue" story, a link in the family chain. I settled back, eager for more. "My grandfather was also my uncle and my aunt was also my cousin." A woman sitting near Timmy nodded sympathetically: "I know, I've got that going on in my family, too."

Wow. I delved back into my training as an estates and trusts lawyer, all those hours painstakingly deciphering charts of lineal descent, but I couldn't figure it out. Was Timmy the product of some Appalachian horror story? I forgot all about the Jewish connection and labored over this new puzzle. I called friends, we drew charts and made spreadsheets until we were blue in the face, and we still couldn't figure it out.

Two weeks went by, and Timmy and I had become buddies. After she had told her story, I mentioned to her that I was Jewish and my mother was from the North, and that broke the ice. She didn't suffer fools gladly and neither did I, so we appreciated that in each other and rolled our eyes in concert when some new idiocy occurred, which was routine at Alexander. Even so, it took me a little while to get up the courage to ask Timmy about her bizarre family tree.

Finally, I just came out with it: "You know, I don't understand what you said about your grandfather and your uncle and your aunt and your cousin, and I am wondering whether I need to worry about you dealing with some incest thing on top of everything else." Timmy laughed. "No." She proceeded to explain something so convoluted that she lost me after thirty seconds. I gave up. She had already moved from potential friend to friend, Jewish or not, incest background or not. I acknowledged the metamorphosis that had taken place, and I enjoyed it tremendously, but I wondered at the time whether this or any other friendship I made at Alexander was going to last. I only had one friend remaining from the number that I had made at Farraday and the same attrition rate seemed likely after I left Alexander.

It's an odd thing, getting to know strangers more intimately in a matter of days than you know your own friends or sometimes even your family. In all three of the facilities in which I spent time, I found that most of the patients talked openly with each other about things that the average person spends a lifetime ducking. To me, the open discussion of our issues felt great. I don't know if it's the Puritan influence in this country or what, but the abject terror which the prospect of openness seems to inspire in many people never ceases to amaze me. My advice: check yourself into a mental institution for a week; the results might surprise you.

CHAPTER TEN

DO NOT DATE ANOTHER PATIENT

O NE RULE THAT IS SET in stone at any psychiatric facility is "no fraternizing among patients." It makes sense, of course; everyone is there to put him or herself back together and barely has the wherewithal to do that, much less what it takes to form a healthy romantic relationship. The staff at Alexander was very strict about it, patrolling the halls to make sure that opposite sex patients were not visiting in each other's rooms and breaking up hugs even if clearly offered only in the spirit of friendship and support.

Naturally, I ignored the rule and did date a fellow patient at Alexander. More accurately, I was flopping around like a wounded mackerel and grabbed the bait when my Romeo cast his line. He looked like an aging Jim Morrison (in fact his name was "Jim") and acted like "Bad" Blake, the main character in the movie *Crazy Heart*. He was larger than life, ridiculously charming and the kind of broken that is fatally attractive to anyone remotely as codependent as I was. He was forty-six versus my fifty-six years old, and since I didn't think I'd ever do more than shake the hand of a man that side of fifty again, that seemed pretty cool. The fact that he was a self-described psychotic, junkie asshole recently diagnosed with narcissistic personality disorder did not disturb me. I had very flexible boundaries at the time.

Jim was a big hit at Alexander. He won the hearts and minds of the people during his tenure there by providing a steady flow of cigarettes. Despite having come in OD'd and in a coma, he had a seemingly limitless supply of cartons, and was compulsively gracious about handing out the cigarettes with which he lined the pockets of his green fleece robe. A secondary market sprang up selling what he gave away, and allegiances came into being, dissolved, and re-formed on a daily basis. The cigarette market worked quite well until Jim got released (a couple of days before me). Then I heard complaints that he had broken his promise to come back and leave a few more cartons. It was odd to see noblesse oblige play out in that setting.

I got out of the inpatient program on a Thursday and Jim came over that night to make dinner. He brought the fixings for veal piccata and pasta with capers, plus wine, roses, chocolates, and gourmet coffee. He brought some pretty good music, too: my first introduction to The Breeders, who I really liked. He stayed over (not much hanky panky), and the next morning things went south.

It turned out that Jim wanted to move in. I had gotten an inkling of this at the hospital, but ignored it, not imagining that he was serious. When I said no and that I had no idea when, if ever, the answer might be yes, at first he got angry. After a while, he started talking about feeling depressed, that life wasn't worth living, and then his language became alarmingly suicidal. I got worried and backpedaled, offering that he could stay with me for a few days if that's what he needed in order to be safe. He declined the offer and wandered off to do something on the computer. He came back and told me that he was arranging to check into Kinnerd, a more upscale hospital in our area. Good, I thought, dealing with a suicidal stranger in my home was not going to be a problem after all.

Still in bed, I sat up and started reading. I vaguely noticed Jim go into the bathroom. I read some more. After a while, a thought flitted through the back my mind: Had Jim been in the bathroom a long time? I dismissed it. A few minutes later, I stirred again. I hadn't heard Jim come out of the bathroom. The apartment seemed very quiet. Too quiet? Out of nowhere, in large letters, came the thought: "IS THERE ANYTHING IN MY BATHROOM THAT SOMEONE COULD USE TO HURT HIMSELF? COULD YOU GET THE BLADE OUT OF A DISPOSABLE RAZOR? IS IT BIG ENOUGH TO CUT YOUR WRISTS WITH?" I got out of bed and walked into the hall. "Jim?" No answer. Louder, close in front of the bathroom door. No answer. I knocked on the door. No answer. Louder. No answer.

I was terrified. The universe slowed down as I opened the bathroom door. As scared as I was, I don't think I expected to have my fears realized, so when I saw Jim floating in the bathtub, time stopped entirely and my head went to yet another universe, the one where the things you see cannot possibly be true, no matter what your eyes tell you. I ran towards the tub, yelling "Jim!" and he sat up. I went to a third universe, the one where dead people sit up. He said, "What's wrong? This is what I do to relax."

I calmed down, he got out of the tub and we were talking, when his phone rang. It was a woman who was still at Alexander in the inpatient program. She was looking for me, frantic. A third friend, a woman who had exhibited only sadness and depression during my stay at the hospital, was bashing her shoulder into the wall, to the point that she was bruised and bloodied, and she kept saying that she wanted to kill herself. Could I talk her down?

So, on day one out of the hospital, I had discovered a naked, suicidal man following his relaxation regimen in my tub and been called upon by a friend who was still "inside" to act as counselor to another patient who was beating herself bloody against the hallway wall of the hospital. I really started to wonder whether my life was imitating Quentin Tarantino's art and if so, why.

CHAPTER ELEVEN

❧

ALL GOD'S CHILLUN' GOT
RELIGION EXCEPT ME

I T CERTAINLY FELT LIKE all God's chillun' had religion except me at Alexander. I got preached to, first-stepped to, serenity-prayed to, invited to church, invited to AA, and invited to every other "A" you could think of. I was happy for the people who had faith. I myself was still searching—along with exactly two other people I met while in treatment. The rest had unshakeable faith in God (you can talk about Higher Power all you want to, these people believed in capital G-O-D). The percentages mystified me. Part of it was clearly rote, an unquestioning allegiance to how people had been raised. Part of it seemed to be necessity being the mother of invention.

Take Perry. Of all the people at Alexander with whom I thought I would never have anything in common, to whom I never expected to speak directly, Perry was number one. A fortyish black crack addict, he wore a pirate's patch over his left eye and was one of the scariest looking people I had ever seen, much less heard. He told of seeing a vision of Jesus Christ encircled in a yellow light one morning at 3:00 a.m. when he was in the ghetto trying to score. The vision coincided with a guy assaulting him with a .357 magnum. Not much mystery there.

The two other people questioning the idea of faith were a white guy in his early thirties, a long time crack addict, and an older black guy, probably in his sixties, the same man whose crack dealer refused to supply him and escorted him back to the hospital campus clean. The young guy was educated, the old guy not in any formal sense, but he was smart and intuitive. Both were introspective and willing to put their questions on the table in front of all of the Bible thumpers. They shared a deep sense of failure that they couldn't believe in God the way everybody else did, particularly the black guy—he was raised devout, but had served in Korea and apparently had seen things that caused his belief system to unravel.

I never stepped up to the plate on this one—I don't know if it's because I was Jewish and didn't want to open that can of worms or that I was already so different from everybody else that I thought my disavowal of formal religion would widen the gap irretrievably.

While I did then and always will consider myself Jewish, by the time I was at Alexander it was no longer a matter of faith, but of background and affiliation. As a child, though, I was a believer, despite the fact that, like my father, I grew up in a *Driving Miss Daisy* kind of world. I'm sure that lots of people who saw the play or the movie thought it was fanciful, but it was not. I grew up exactly like that, to the letter. Jewish though we were, I celebrated only Christmas, never Hanukkah, always had a tree with a big angel on top, and my mother bought only the most delicate, stunning ornaments at Bergdorf Goodman. I am pretty sure we had a manger scene, but memory may not be serving me on that one. We observed certain holidays, like Passover, but for our convenience we moved it to the nearest Saturday night, irrespective of the day on which it fell.

Maybe as a result of that upbringing, I had a fairly jaundiced view of organized religion, whatever its origin, and nothing ever happened since my younger days to give me reason to change my thinking. I remember one particular incident involving the rabbi who officiated at the

Bar Mitzvah of a close friend's child. I had traveled a long way to be part of the ceremony and as an honor and mark of my closeness to the family I was invited up to the podium to participate. I was not then a spiritual person, not seeking it, not missing it, but I had seen and read enough to have a passing understanding of religion, spirituality, ritual, and tradition. Although I was not Bat Mitzvahed (girls did not participate in that tradition when I was growing up), I well understood the gravity of this rite of passage for my friend's son, and took it very seriously. In addition, I had been told that the rabbi who was officiating was a much admired man, loved for his kindness and compassion, so I was looking forward to hearing what he would have to say.

Imagine my surprise when, during the ceremony, I overheard the following conversation between the rabbi and my friend, the father of the Bar Mitzvah boy. The Rabbi's opening gambit: "So, I've heard that you're moving to Pennsylvania?" "Yes, Rabbi," my friend responded, attempting to peer around the rabbi for a glimpse of his son, who was speaking from the pulpit. Next move from the Rabbi: "I guess you are selling your house here, then?" "Yes, Rabbi." Closing gambit: "My wife, Beverly, is a real estate agent, a good one, and I am sure she would be happy to help you with the sale of your house." The Rabbi may have offered to give my friend his wife's card; I'm not sure. I thought to myself, if this was the best of the best, the holiest of the holy, and that's what he has to say at one of the most solemn and meaningful moments in my friend's life, then cut me loose, give me a shaman in the jungle and call it a day.

Religion, for me, was a bumpy road from the start. Like other Jewish children of my generation who were raised in a mostly secular household, I did attend Sunday School. My parents cut me all kinds of slack there since they didn't place any importance on religious education, and I took full advantage, cutting classes, sassing the teachers and ignoring my studies. I came away knowing nothing about the Jewish faith, but I got an interesting glimpse into the cultural set-up of Jewish life in Atlanta in the 1950s and '60s. I was shocked to find that there were Jewish kids in my Sunday School class, people my own age, who lived on the other side of town, which up until then I had only known as the mysterious place to which we traveled once a year for a Jewish holiday meal with some really old people, parents of friends of my parents. When I say they were really old, I mean they were Biblical, and the ones whom I remember best were the zaftig old ladies with the Russian (or Polish or Lithuanian) accents who sat with their legs open so that you could see where their stockings rolled up just above their knees.

I found it at once frightening and thrilling that kids my age also lived over there, outside the walls, so to speak, and survived just fine. My parents' group had made that quick immigrant transition to the other side of town, from outsider to insider, from Russian, Polish and Yiddish to flawless English, and I viewed the old section as an outlaw place, wild and woolly, a place unknown and unwelcoming to me. The truth was that I was jealous of these kids: they so clearly *belonged* in that place—it fit them to a "T"— while I was the perennial outsider wherever I was, especially once my parents transferred me in seventh grade to a new school where I was the only Jewish person in my class.

It's not like my old school was a rabbinic seminary; it also was a Christian preparatory school, and in Chapel, held first thing every morning, I learned to love hymns like "Onward Christian Soldiers" and "Rock of Ages" and even did my duty as an acolyte from time to time. Still, there was a small crowd of Jewish kids there, and while my friends were both Jewish and non-Jewish, I always knew that my compatriots were there. Not so at the new school, where I studied Old Testament and New Testament with the cream of young gentile society, on their way to cotillion and their debuts. My mother warned me in tenth grade that my new friends would drop me when it got closer to the time of these social rites of passage, and she was right about all except one.

It was in eleventh grade at this second school that I got my religious baptism by fire. At Friday morning assembly there was generally a program that started out secular at 9:00 a.m. and turned religious around about 9:45 a.m. Example: a college football coach would come and talk inspirationally about football, but all of a sudden we'd be hearing about those great big goalposts in the sky, and then Jesus would come into it and the gloves were off for real, and we'd get a good old-fashioned Bible-thumping rant.

So on this one day in the spring of 1969, imagine a folk singer instead of a football coach, and he starts out really cool, all mellow-voiced and hip. Glance at your watch, and you can time the shift, now we are into heavy Deep Southern Fundamentalism, in favor at the time and known for its literal application of scripture. As juniors, we were invited to meet the singer privately in the formal Communal Room, and to ask him questions and chat with him. As the discussion got more and more radical, I grew more uncomfortable. Finally, I couldn't resist the urge to speak up and ask him what he thought about someone like me, Jewish, a non-believer in Christ, much less the brand of Christianity that he was hawking. Without missing a beat, he said, "You will burn in Hell unless you accept Jesus Christ as your Lord and Savior!" We went at it for a few minutes, him ranting at me and me fighting back, but he wouldn't back off and I started retreating, shocked and confused. Growing up in the South and being, in the year 1969, the only Jewish person in my class, it wasn't as if I had never heard an ugly remark about my faith, but never anything so extreme and never had I been so visibly singled out, as if I were going to be cut from the herd and branded or worse.

I may not have learned anything in Sunday School, but neither had I ever questioned that my belief in the Jewish religion was valid, nor had anyone else ever done that for me. This folk singer/preacher/fanatic had opened a door for me, and I tumbled through it. At that moment I lost the blind faith of a child, but I had nothing with which to replace it, and I broke down and cried.

The school authorities must have been scared senseless. After I ran crying to my Bible teacher, she sent me to one of the deans, who sent me home with the most popular girl in our class, the doyenne of the debutante bunch, to be cosseted and comforted until my threat level could be assessed and contained and I was deemed safe to send back to my house. At about 6:00 p.m., I returned home, still shaken and upset, and sought out my mother, as usual at this time of day lying on her chaise longue, shadows lengthening in her bedroom, reading a book. (Chaises longues are an oddly recurring image in my life.)

She put the book to the side and leaned back, seemingly attentive to my story. Finally, I wound down and stopped talking, waiting for a response. I never got one. My mother (both parents, actually) was so disengaged from all except the most secular aspects of religion that she could not relate to my tale and it triggered no reaction in her at all. I don't know if she even discussed the incident with my father, because it was never mentioned again between us. I'm sure that the school administrators were tickled that they never heard a word from my parents. I wonder what defenses they had assembled by the following Monday morning when I returned to school, nothing changed, invisible once again to my newfound debutante friend.

I was, of course, still Jewish by birth after that, but not by religion, which I lost that that day, and it took me many years of wandering in the desert to find something to replace it.

PART TWO

SHAPING SUZY

CHAPTER TWELVE

SECRETS, LIES, AND NO VIDEOTAPE

I GREW UP IN A FAMILY FULL OF SECRETS. I participated in our hidden secrets and myths, conforming not only my actions but my very thoughts to the sole end of maintaining our family's public face. It went against the grain, but when I was a child, doing otherwise did not seem like an option. I was afraid that no one would love me if I pointed out the truths that we so studiously avoided. This fear was not unfounded, since it was made clear to me early on that none of what I felt inside was permitted to be verbalized to either of my parents. There was no guessing about it with my mother, who told me openly and directly, "You are not allowed to get angry with me," with the further and disastrous implication for my developing ego that I wasn't allowed either to express or even to *feel* any other negative emotion. The fact that she was extremely angry when she said it reinforced the fact all of the power resided with her. She could do and say as she pleased; it was only I who was impotent. Although my father didn't voice it, I felt the same taboo with him. The effect of being forced to shut down so completely at a young age was profound. The secrets formed around me in layers, until I felt as if I was buried within them, all but completely stifled.

It didn't occur to me until years after I saw the movie how critical the idea of the videotape was to *Sex, Lies, and Videotape,* a mostly forgotten film starring James Spader, king of the mainstream kinky movie genre. Secrets aren't secret anymore if you catch them on camera, especially if you go public with them. That takes away their power, but sometimes it requires guts to do it, more guts than I possessed for a long time.

I did not have a videotape or a camera, but I did have a memory, with all of the dots already connected; it's just that I was afraid to use it for many years. It took a long time for the fear that I would lose my family's love if I questioned the system to subside enough for me to look at the reality that had shaped my life. I not only skirted, denied and ignored that reality, but I convinced myself that the family myths were true, which allowed me to actively and vocally uphold them in public, as if my life depended on it, which in some way I must have felt that it did.

What caused all the wreckage? What was the big secret? Was I molested as a child, injured in some horrific and irreparable way? No, although for much of the 1980s I thought that something along those lines must have happened. I had very few memories of my childhood and youth, and it was in vogue at the time to explain such lapses as blocked memories of sexual abuse. After years of exploration, including a number of desperate phone interviews that must have greatly puzzled my former nursemaid Amelia and her daughter Pamela, I came to realize that growing up in a family like mine was injury enough.

The simple truth is that I was shaped from a very young age by a sense of abandonment and betrayal, and the magnitude of neither was small. I spent years coming to terms with the abandonment, with the fact that even without Amelia's inexplicable disappearance when I was thirteen, to have been raised from birth to age thirteen by her and not my own mother was abandonment enough. I remember being confused as a child when my parents yelled at me for calling Amelia "Mama," having no clue that she wasn't. From the time I could speak my mother instructed me to call her "Honey," as she had done with my brother before me, and in my life I was never invited to call my mother by any name that would pass for maternal. I have heard it said that the abandonment was extreme because my parents traveled for long stretches, leaving my brother and me behind, but that's not the reason. From an emotional standpoint I felt at least as abandoned in their presence as I did when they were gone.

Strange that it took me so long to accept that I had suffered abandonment as a child—it was never a secret to even the most casual of bystanders, that's how obvious it was. Not so for the betrayals: they weren't obvious, and no one else knew about them except the few friends whom I told over the years.

While everyone endures countless little betrayals in his or her life, they generally pass by with the smallest of ripples. Most people also suffer accretive betrayals, the ones that accumulate over time, until you realize that you can no longer count on someone who used to have your back. It hurts, but you come to terms with it. Then there's the kind of betrayal that is like a harpoon in your gut, huge and sudden and sharp. I was betrayed in this fashion more than once, and the impact stayed with me.

In 1969, at age sixteen, in the midst of an angry scene with my mother, I gathered my courage and said to her, "I think I need to see a psychiatrist." Her response was to slap me full across the face and to tell me that we handled our problems in private. I took that to the bank, not mentioning it again, until some time in my early twenties when I spoke to my father in desperation, having suffered in the intervening years a number of bouts of depression. Uncharacteristically, he gave me the name of a psychiatrist without telling my mother. I saw the man twice—it was not a good fit—and I did not try again until I was in my late twenties, after which I took charge of my choices in that arena.

The next time I broached my psychological issues to my family was in 1990 and I was thirty-six years old, driving back with my mother from a visit to the pediatrician with my two-year-old son. I said: "I think I have problems with depression." She said: "I don't know what that is," and changed the subject. Skip to the year 2000. I was forty-seven years old and had just spent three weeks in an eating disorders program (remember, the one that I thought was going to be like Weight Watchers?). The night of my release I called my parents and asked if I could come over to talk to them about something important. I explained where I had been for three weeks and that I thought that they should know about it. Their collective response: "Oh, we were afraid that you were coming to tell us that you were going to get a divorce." End of discussion, no questions asked.

"So what's the big deal?" you might ask. Typical of some people of that generation, everything was swept under the rug, no dirty laundry was inspected, no unpleasantness admitted or discussed. True, and that's how I viewed it as well, not happily, but realistically.

Until the depth and breadth of at least one parent's pathology finally was revealed, a couple of years after my release from Farraday. Unable to remain silent on the topic any longer, my mother raised the issue of my significant weight gain in the preceding months (increasing from a size 6/8 to a 12/14): "What happened to you? You were so thin!" Me: "You wouldn't want me to lose weight the way I did. I lost all of that weight before I had to go to Farraday because I was so sick." Her response: "Yes, I would." Me, feeling the world start to tilt: "No, you really wouldn't want that, you don't understand, not that way, not for me to be that sick, you must not have heard what I said." Final answer: "Yes I would."

I shouldn't have been surprised. As a child, around seven years old, I was not particularly overweight, but not a twig either, about average. My mother, obsessed with my size, would routinely grab me by the elbow and drag me from my room through her dressing room, into her bathroom and finally onto her scale. Years later, I can still feel the hard pinch of her hand around my elbow, the sensation as she pulled my body alongside hers that she was all angles and bones, nothing round. I could feel the weight of her eyes for sure. One of our maids used to have a phrase for their rage-filled impact: "when those blue eyes turn black." As my mother dragged me I would cry and I would protest, "No, I haven't gained any weight," despite the fact that I was always hoarding candy bars and eating them in secret. Of course I had gained weight and of course I lied; I was scared shitless of her wrath. Even that young I knew that she was capable of laying into me with a tongue-lashing that would rip my skin off. And when the scale revealed that I had indeed gained a pound or two, she would do exactly that.

The scale episodes had a lasting impact on my life. As a teenager, I would race into the bathroom, rip off all of my clothes and jump on the scale. If I didn't like what I saw, I would shift my weight around to see if I could get the needle to move a quarter or even an eighth of a pound lower. I did this four to six times a day. My mood would swing from one end of the spectrum to the other based on the result. Bad result, I fell into the abyss. Good result, I was soaring. Throughout high school, my self-image was a product of the uncaring calculations of my scale. At college, I didn't own a scale, but I would use someone else's from time to time and if I weighed more than I thought I did, any happy feelings I had died on the spot. Later in my life, I realized how self-defeating this compulsion was, and after a few false starts, I gave up scales entirely. I have not voluntarily known my weight for fifteen years, since the birth of my last child. When I go for a physical exam, I tell the nurse that I do not want to see or be told my weight, nor do I want her accidentally to show me the chart or make a comment about my weight, even if it is positive. I do not say it casually; I am extremely forceful in making my wishes known and always say it at least twice so that there is no mistaking my intentions. Even so, it is amazing how difficult it seems for these trained professionals to resist brightly informing me, "Oh, you've lost weight!" or "Whoops, up a few pounds!" The last time this happened it was the doctor who looked at my chart and said, "It's lower than it was last year!" right on the heels of my polite yet unequivocal instruction not to comment on my weight. I guess that even with their training, medical professionals are not immune to our national fixation on body size, which I find an interesting cultural commentary when I get over wanting to punch them in the face.

I ingested my mother's early criticism of my appearance to the degree that irrespective of how I really looked, for most of my life the only goddess I saw reflected in the mirror was the Venus of Willendorf, with whom I unhappily identified from the first time I came across her in the art history courses I took in college. She was one of the earliest sculptures made by modern man, short and round with a Buddha belly. Described that way, she sounds kind of cute, certainly not hideous or repulsive to look at, but that was my take on both the hapless Venus and myself. That for most of my life I looked nothing like her, and instead, by all objective reports, ranged from attractive to quite pretty or even beautiful, was completely irrelevant. I viewed my face and my body with overwhelming disgust, exceeded only by the outrage that I felt that the simple gift of living comfortably inside my own skin in a physical sense had been stolen from me so young and so painfully.

Appearances were everything to both of my parents, and that was the family altar upon which I sacrificed myself for most of my life. If there are religious overtones to this statement, it is no accident, because in my family how you looked *was* the Bible, and I bought into it lock, stock, and barrel. It took me a long time to achieve any degree of recovery from this pathology, long into my adulthood, long into and after my marriage and long past my child-rearing years. I was not the quickest learner when it came to these particular lessons.

CHAPTER THIRTEEN

LESSONS FROM THE MENAGERIE

ALTHOUGH I WAS SOMETIMES (always?) unsure of my mother's feelings for people (me?), there was never any doubt about her feelings for animals—she loved them unequivocally. First and foremost there was our long parade of dogs: Sambo, Tar Baby (yes, these were black poodles, weren't the 1950s grand?), Booboo, Jenny, Nanny, Mac, Fred, Anastasia, Merry, Amethyst, Chanel, Chanel II, Sophia, Loren (yellow lab sisters named after the actress), Ethel, Choco, Carmel and Lauren. I personally christened Chitch, Molada and Melissa, the threesome of alley cats who hung around the back door. Amelia, my nursemaid, had her own cats, Pearl and Flossie.

While I have no particular desire to make every mundane spousal negotiation between my parents a Machiavellian manipulation, it often seemed so to me, raised as I was listening to mother's insistence that men were made to be molded and it was a wife's job to do it properly and to her advantage. One of the more instructive things I witnessed as a child was my mother giving Fred, our first miniature Italian greyhound (aka MIG, not to be confused with the Russian aircraft) to my father for his birthday. The fourteen-pound quivering muzzle on stilts that she thrust into his arms was my mother's baby, with a price tag that he would have rejected out of hand had she asked him to purchase it for her. But she was smarter than that: she presented it as a gift to him, with impenetrable enthusiasm and a "Happy Birthday!!" that brooked no resistance. He played along, bemused but willing, a movable object meeting an irresistible force. He made a couple of weak jokes and handed Fred back to my mother, to whom the animal promptly attached itself for the duration of its life.

The next Italian greyhound, Anastasia, was a real winner; she contracted some kind of bacterial disease in her middle years and lost a third of one side of her jaw (her tongue hung out of her mouth sideways), half of one of her back legs and a third of one of her front legs. It is my recollection that she was missing part of yet another leg, but realistically I don't think she could have stood up. She shivered through even the hottest of summer months and in winter slept on top of our poodle of the moment, like one of those parasite fish that attaches itself to a shark.

Nurtured by my mother like the last dodo bird on Earth, Anastasia made it to a ripe old age, but at some point we were all aware that she was about to go. My mother sat on the floor and held her and cried and cried, for two solid days as it turned out. I never saw her cry over anything else like that and at the time I didn't understand it, railed against it, that she could show so much emotion over a dog but so little to me. I later came to understand her better, to accept her guarded ways and to pay more attention to her deeds, some of which turned out to be quite spectacular as they concerned me.

As for my own pets, they have not been as numerous or varied as the animals of my youth, but they have had their own stories and their own impact on my life. The first dog of my married years looked like a winged monkey from *The Wizard of Oz*, prompting my mother to exclaim, upon first introduction, in best Bette Davis voice, "Wahht is thahht??!" Other notable pets included Carrie, the Schipperke who, just like me, was a thin person on the inside, and Marx, a Wire Fox Terrier who bore an uncanny resemblance to my ex-husband, Leo, both in musculature (wiry) and temperament (Tasmanian Devil). These two moved with the family to Hong Kong, enduring four weeks of quarantine during which my familiar ate the bulk of Marx's food, emerging more robust than ever while poor Marx came back little more than a skeleton, requiring careful nursing to return to health.

I remember when my cousin, Erin, was divorced many years ago and after a time acquired two small Chihuahuas, I warned her, "Don't become one of those divorced women who talks about her dogs all the time and relates to them more than she does to people." Erin either paid close attention to me or was never at risk, for she leads a full and varied life, while the "cat lady" in me seemed often to be pounding at the door.

Who was I kidding? The cat lady in me wasn't pounding at the door, she was out; in fact she had been out for a long time. She had wreaked havoc with my household, even down to my own pets, poor things, although my current dog, Henrietta, arrived with her own baggage. From the get go, Henrietta, was neurotic, filled with separation anxiety. They said at the SPCA that she had been returned three times because she was too needy. We took her anyway, Leo, the three kids and I, and by the time I got divorced and brought her with me to live on my own, she was pretty well wrecked and so was I.

She cried when I left the house and she cried when I got back home. In fact, she cried more then than at any other time. The pleasure of seeing me mixed with the worry that I would go away again was too much for her. She tore clothes from hangers and dragged them around the house while I was at work and she nipped at my face when I got home at night, she was that distraught. I would arrange for her to have easy access to the kitchen garbage in the hopes that tearing through boxes and balled up dinner napkins would satisfy her and she would leave my closets alone. (It was an old house and none of the doors would close properly, so locking up the clothes wasn't an option.) It didn't work. I couldn't blame her if she hated being alone; so did I.

By the fall of 2005 I was in the throes of divorce hell, and Henrietta was taking it hard. You never saw a sadder looking, more insecure dog. I was in the middle of a God-awful regimen of repeating positive affirmations to myself, day after day, night after night: "I love and accept myself." "I am a good mother." "My self-esteem is not negotiable." It wasn't working on me, but for some reason I thought, "Why not try this on Henrietta?" Happy Dog Therapy was born.

I sat Henrietta across from me on the bed and looked hard into her eyes. I summoned every ounce of enthusiasm I could muster and said, in a voice you would use to a not terribly bright three-year-old: "Who's Happy Dog??!! Who's a Happy Girl??!! She's so Happy!!! What a Happy Dog!!!! Is that Happy Dog?? Yes, she is, she is so Happy!!!!" I scrunched my face up, I beamed, I trilled the phrases, over and over. I have a very deep voice that does not project well and I had to work hard to maintain a level of screechy good humor, ignoring that my voice was starting to rasp and my throat hurt.

At first, nothing. Then she stood up and smiled (anyone who has a dog knows what this looks like). A little light came on in her eyes and she wagged her tail. Victory! Now, any time Henrietta gets depressed, we do Happy Dog Therapy.

I tried it on my cat, Horace, but he was impervious. That's too bad because I think he could have used it. I'm pretty sure that Henrietta and I had started to wear on him.

CHAPTER FOURTEEN

HORACE'S NINE LIVES

My cat, Horace, is extraordinary. He was born in 2005 from a feral cat who brought herself into a horse barn just in time to deliver her litter. It was a bitterly cold February morning, and Horace and one other kitten were frozen solid by the time the stable hands came in to feed the horses. They put the two kittens in their pockets and eventually brought both back to life, just like the puppy in *101 Dalmatians*. So, one life for Horace was used up at birth; eight to go.

Before Horace, I hadn't had a cat for more than two decades. The last one had been my grandmother's. In my late twenties and living alone, I took Vinnie in rather than let her be put down after my grandmother died. I didn't much like Vinnie, and my Shih Tzu, Ming, hated her. I didn't like him either for any of the eleven years I owned him, so that made the circle complete. I often complained to my mother about Vinnie, but figured there was no way around it. My mother had four dogs and at the time my brother was not a cat person. Oddly, he is now; I guess we all come to it in time.

I complained about Vinnie steadily for four months and then, when I came home one day from work, she was missing. I looked everywhere, but she didn't turn up. I wasn't worried, but I was puzzled. I called my mother to tell her what was going on. While at the time my mother held the place of highest honor in my pantheon of demons, I had a coterminous need for her to be my friend and confidante.

"Oh, I came by and got Vinnie, took her to the vet and had her put down." I didn't believe her, but it was true. If I were to remind my mother of this story today, more than twenty years later, she still wouldn't know why what she did was wrong. For my part, I shouldn't have been surprised, since I knew that my mother had her own code, strongly held though mostly a mystery to me. In a different age she would have been President of the United States, and when you hear the expression "timing is everything," believe it, because I have no doubt that she would have hit the red button and that would have been that.

I owned quite a few dogs over the next twenty years, but never another cat until Horace. Over the course of time, he has gotten soft through indulgence, but for his first several years he was a real he-man of a cat, the neighborhood stud. When I walked Henrietta, he would always come with us, following behind and slightly to the side. In every place that I have lived since I owned him, the neighbors have met me through Horace, charmed by the sight of him strolling along on our walks. He used up his second life locked in the cellar of one of those neighbors for a day and a half. The only reason he got rescued is that another neighbor later remembered noticing him in the yard when the cellar door was flipped open.

In 2009 I moved back south, right back in with my parents, then eighty-nine and eighty-four years old. They lived on the eighth floor of an apartment building with their middle-aged poodle, Carmel. What little personality remained to Carmel when we arrived was decimated when Horace took up residence—he was too alien a presence to be borne by such an inbred sensibility. To spare Carmel's feelings, Horace, the King of the 'Hood, was confined to my room. That's when he started to use up his remaining seven lives, fast, with some help from me that would have been better withheld.

I felt terrible about Horace's confinement, and started wondering about the balcony outside of my room. It was a spacious balcony with a high wall, almost up to my chest, and a broad ledge. Horace was so unhappy that one day I gave in to the impulse. He draped his body around the open door and stepped out onto a paver. Then, as any cat person would have expected, he jumped up on the ledge. I am not a cat person. Horace showed up late in my life, when the entity that had decided that zero was too low for me to go felt that it was time to throw me a bone.

I knew enough about animals in general not to lunge, so I turned my back on Horace and slid down the wall onto the stone floor, sitting almost under his perch. Time started up again when I heard a thud next to me, after what could have been minutes but was probably no more than ten seconds. This time I did lunge, got Horace in a stranglehold that would have made Jesse Ventura proud, threw him back in my room and slammed the door. After a few minutes, I had recovered enough to get curious, and I went to the computer and googled something like "apartment+balcony+cat."

Results came back for "high-rise syndrome," describing other cats that had launched themselves into space from as high as the forty-sixth story in pursuit of birds or other distractions, and, amazingly, survived. It was comforting to know that I'd had a passing shot at pulling this ox out of the ditch no matter what. Back-up plans play a big role in my psyche, since, as any perfectionist will tell you, if you have half a brain and some creativity, it's hard to be wrong on the fifth try.

Horace was down to six lives, and I started looking for alternatives. Friends with yards were a possibility, and the same cousin who later carted off my mini-blender as a potential instrument of suicide agreed to let me use her house as Horace's new base of operations. The first visit was painful: Horace disappeared for three hours and I was worried sick, sure that he would never find his way back. He did, and weekly visits to Cousin Erin's were built into my routine. They were a pleasant escape for me as well, because at this time my father was living in the apartment under hospice care with round-the-clock nurses, my mother was consumed with the details of his care, and I was playing the supporting role to them both.

One summer day, with the temperature in the 90s, I put Horace in his crate and headed over to Cousin Erin's. As usual, he hated being in the crate and got louder and louder in his complaints. I let him out after a couple of minutes. I am a pushover for kids and animals—I am the original "No, No, No, No, Yes" mother, which in retrospect I do not recommend as a parenting style. (Can I have it?

No. I want it! No. Why can't I have it? You just can't/I said no/Because I said so. Why won't you let me have it? I just won't. Mom!!! No! Please???? No! Please??? OK, I guess so, I mean just for a while, here, just take it!) I am no different with my animals: I do not easily resist their demands, even if it means that I have to drive with a cat under my brakes.

With Horace no longer making a disturbance, I drove on, radio on low, daydreaming a little as I went. After a few minutes, a voice in my head started telling me something, but I didn't pay attention right away. After another minute, I realized that something had changed in the car. There was a sound that shouldn't be there, but what was it? I finally caught up to my surroundings and put my finger on the fact that air was coming in the back window, more specifically the back window that I hadn't opened. I turned all the way around and looked in the back seat, dreading what I would see, hoping that the gods of timing were on my side and that I was being allowed to intervene after Horace put the window down but before he jumped, as I knew he would. Nope, I was too late to the party.

The first thing I did was to pull over, roll all the windows up and curse the Universe at the top of my lungs. Next, I called my daughter, Juliana, who had come with Rachel to live with me for the summer, and we printed two hundred flyers and nailed them up in the area where I thought

Horace might have gotten out. People were home from work and there were loads of runners and walkers, a number of whom stopped. One man told Juliana about an email group and gave her the address to which to send information about Horace to be circulated among the neighborhood members. We went right home and sent an email and a photo.

The very next day I got a response about a cat that a lady had seen under a car several streets from where I thought Horace had disappeared. I went over right away, and while I didn't find Horace, I posted more flyers. Days went by, and we all started to think that this story wasn't going to have a happy ending. I was shell shocked, still off balance from the preceding months: August '08—leave East Coast treatment facility after ten weeks; February '09—quit work; April '09—pack up and store most of my belongings and, jobless and homeless, move back to my old hometown and into my parents' apartment; June '09—watch my father's slow, bedridden decline following a broken hip from a fall.

I walked into the apartment on a Sunday in July nine days after Horace disappeared. I noticed a slip of paper with a nearby address sitting on a chair in the foyer. I took note of it, out of place as it was, and the thought flitted through my head that maybe it had something to do with Horace, no sooner thought than dismissed. I opened the door to my bedroom. One daughter had Horace in her arms and the other was filming my reaction. I grabbed Horace and swung him around. He seemed happy to see me, and certainly no worse for the wear, exactly four ounces thinner, according to the vet the next day. A couple had seen the email about a missing cat, noticed Horace hanging around and managed to get the number from his tag. Four lives gone, five to go.

I moved out in November 2009 to an apartment with a doggy door, so Horace resumed his role as ruler of all he surveyed, and I no longer had to plan his outings. It was a ratty apartment in a questionable neighborhood, but it was all that I could afford. I spent a lot of time being scared in that apartment, scared that someone would break down the door and rape me or worse, scared that I would have to live in that kind of place for the rest of my life, scared that my life would never change.

Then again, fear was nothing new to me.

CHAPTER FIFTEEN

FEAR

I GREW UP FLYING on propeller planes which, limited by the technology of the time, flew straight through thunder storms, lightning all around. It was spectacular and I loved every minute of it, had no fear at all when the pilot invited me into the cockpit for a look out front. Fear didn't come until I was in my early twenties flying trans-Atlantic, which was not a new experience for me and should have been copacetic. I stood up to stretch next to the back porthole window, glanced out, and froze. I have no idea what happened to me in that moment, but abject terror took root and continued unabated for years, only retreating, marginally, in my late forties.

On one of the early white-knuckle flights following that day, a mantra came to me: "God will not let me die until I have had the perfect orgasm." That this became a fundamental, unshakeable tenet of my belief system was striking in its hopefulness. Prior to that time, I had not had any orgasm, much less a perfect one, a source of great consternation to me, product of the sexual revolution that I was. I had tried and failed, more than once. If I had known how to interpret my early experiences of lack of nurturance and failed attachment, I would have known that frigidity would be a given for me, but I didn't, and I don't know what I would have done differently except fret even more.

It didn't help that I was woefully uneducated: as a sophomore in college, I told the upperclassman who was attempting to relieve me of my virginity that we didn't have enough time left, it was 4:00 a.m. and I had class at 8:00. He proved me wrong and I made class by about three hours and fifty-one minutes. Sadly, the other nine minutes were a lot less fun than I had hoped.

Consistent with that inauspicious beginning, I followed up with thirteen years of terrible sex but marvelously safe airplane travel. Seatbelts were wasted on me and as for the oxygen mask, I could have happily supplied the nearest traveling pet. Then I got married to Leo and as with most newlyweds, the sex was dandy initially. It later soured, distracted as we were by jobs, raising children, the pursuit of money, dinner parties, and countless other things. Our divorce liberated us both from that difficulty, among others, but for me, brought an unexpected predicament in its place. The problem was that, flotsaming and jetsaming around as recently divorced women tend to do, I started to have really good sex. No, I take that back. It wasn't really good sex, it was great sex, sitting in my car, at my desk at work, with a guy, without a guy, nighttime, daytime, anytime and all the time. The orgasms were simultaneous and multiple, replete with fireworks—in a word, much as I would have preferred to dodge it, perfect. Therein lay the rub. If God wouldn't let me die until I'd had the perfect orgasm, well, God was now officially off the hook and I was on my own in the friendly skies. What to do?

Face my fear. Gag. Double gag. I loathed the idea of facing my fears, I would not do it, Sam I Am, I would not do it for a ham, I would not do it in a jam, I would not do it, Sam I Am. I had read years before about a guy with an eating disorder who got over it by "facing his fears." He sat up all night through the waves of fear and anger and self loathing and whatever else came up, and by morning he had turned the corner. I remember thinking, "Wow, one night, that's all it took, I can do that." As it turned out, I couldn't. Not one night, not one hour, hardly ten minutes when the going got really rough.

So here was the real fear: suppose I was born without the wherewithal to "do" life, either born without it or, more likely, had it knocked out of me through some combination of nature and nurture? Nurture, huh? Translation: parenting. Which parent? Both? Not to my way of thinking, not for a long time. My father, in the manner of the men of his socio-economic class in his generation, passed all child-rearing decisions to my mother, so for years, as White Knight to her Black Queen, he was exempt from my resentments, while my mother became my finest obsession.

Until the day I went to a funeral in the summer of 2010. A pillar of the Jewish community had died, and my mother invited me to go with her and my brother, if I felt so inclined. I did feel inclined, and I wondered why. I had hardly known the man, had been friends with his daughter a long time back, but hadn't seen her for years. I went anyway, and I heard the same things that I had heard at recent funerals of elder statesmen in the Jewish community, and it hurt, each time it had hurt and it did this time as well. For what I heard was celebrations of what the now grown children had learned from their fathers, from jokes about where to sit at a funeral (near the air conditioning), to the proper uses of money (for health, welfare and enjoyment, and then for helping others), to imprecations against grieving overmuch after their deaths, to global topics such as the importance of family, the meaning of friendship and the significance of community.

These funerals pointed up with painful clarity what those other children had received from their fathers that I had missed. As a child, my father taught me exactly three things that I remember. One: always look someone in the eye when you speak to them. Two: always grip someone's hand firmly when you shake it—there is nothing worse than having a grip like a dead fish. Three: drive defensively. Other things he must have taught me by example; he certainly was a kind person, quite popular in the community, known for his superior golfing ability (he had a zero handicap in his heyday) and his quick wit.

I was a Daddy's girl growing up and even into my twenties. My mother used to remark with some envy that I had him wrapped around my little finger. There was an implication that I had done this on purpose, but it wasn't the case. It was a natural thing. We were the pair in the family who gravitated toward peace and harmony and away from confrontation, so our alignment was to be expected. I believed in our bond, trusted it, trusted him. It was the Suzy thing to do. I still carry the scars.

More than anything my father taught me by commission, the biggest lesson he taught me was by omission: when the chips are down and the shit has hit the fan, you are on your own. The cavalry will not be coming to save you.

A case in point: when I was sixteen years old, my mother, father and I were driving from Miami to Palm Beach for dinner with some relatives. My mother and I got into a discussion about the Vietnam War (the year was 1969) and I said that if I were eligible for the draft, I would not fight; I would go to Canada instead. I am sure that I was parroting the popular catechism of my generation, but in part I meant it. I had always had a firm grip on the concepts of war and death, positive that I wanted no part of either.

My mother lost it. "YOUR GRANDFATHER GROVELED IN THE DIRT SO YOU COULD LIVE IN THIS COUNTRY!!!!! WHO DO YOU THINK YOU ARE, YOU LITTLE TIN JESUS??!!!" This was the one and only time I heard of my grandfather groveling anywhere; to my knowledge he was a successful real estate investor who lived first in Brooklyn and, by the time my mother was in her early twenties, on Central Park West. Her diatribe continued all the way to Palm Beach where, in a theatrical move atypical of my mother, she sat in the car while my father and I joined the rest of the family in the restaurant for dinner. By this time I was crying inconsolably, but after the first Scotch of my life went down like Kool-Aid, I recovered some portion of my tattered equilibrium.

My mother stayed in the car for the entire meal, resisting all attempts to persuade her to abandon the parking lot in favor of the dinner table. After dinner, I went back out to the car with some trepidation, but, fortified by the Scotch, also hopeful that my mother's tantrum had spent itself. If anything, she was more tuned up. She ranted and raved, and I was reduced to rubble and then from rubble to powder. All the while, my father sat quiet. It was only at the tail end of the trip, about an hour and fifteen minutes in, that he spoke three uninflected words intended, it would appear, to dam the flood: "Now, that's enough." Another torrent from her. Again, him, even more softly: "It's water under the bridge now, leave it alone." She rolled right over him, as if he hadn't spoken.

By the time the drive ended and my mother stopped raging of her own accord, I was catatonic, the emotional equivalent of a veal chop that had been pounded to a schnitzel. If I hadn't known it before, I should have known then that I had no champion, but I couldn't admit it. Because if I didn't have him, then all I had was me, and that wasn't enough.

My father had an odd background. His brother was a bona fide genius, in the Guinness Book of Records as the youngest person at the time to have gone to college, at age eleven. My father was in many ways as smart as his brother, particularly when it came to anything mathematical. He used to add columns of numbers eight wide and twelve long in his head, just for fun, and I always thought it was a shame that the calculator came along to spoil his good times. Even though he was so bright, my grandparents decided not to put another child through the social discomfort of being in college as a pre-teen.

My father's father was a character, and tales of his exploits abounded. He would go to the funerals of strangers for entertainment. He over tipped for bad service, something no one understood. My father used to say that you never wanted to come up behind his father without letting him know that you were there: he would react by hitting first and asking questions later. This was not the only story I heard about my grandfather being violent. Apparently, he alone was allowed to speak at the dinner table, and my father told me more than once about his father "slugging" a young cousin who made the mistake of interrupting my grandfather at dinner. Based on these and similar stories, I got the sense that my grandfather was not a nurturing presence in my father's life. But I also know that he was very proud of my father's golfing ability and used to follow my father at the tournaments in which he played, hiding behind trees in the gallery so that he wouldn't be a distraction.

My grandfather was unique as a public figure as well as a private person. He was a legend in the community for his philanthropy and if my grandmother hadn't held the purse strings tightly, he would have given away everything they had. As a teenager, when I would sign a check, many a merchant would look at my name, make the connection and share that my grandfather had given him the money to get started in business. He never asked for the money back, because in his view it wasn't a loan. If the money was in his pocket it was there to be given freely. He was viewed as judge and jury in the business that he built, and often dispensed marital and child-rearing advice to his employees.

Funny how things work their way down through generations. I believe that my father was able to tolerate the harsher aspects of my mother (temper, intransigence) because he had been conditioned to them by exposure to his father. I was able to tolerate some of the same characteristics in Leo because of my earlier exposure to my mother. I sometimes wondered whether anyone could ever escape that kind of conditioning and worried that the efforts I made to interrupt the cycle with my own children were in vain. After that funeral in the summer of 2010, I asked my youngest daughter whether she had learned anything from me during her life. Long suffering, she said "yes," reminding me that I asked the same question about once a week. Of this I had no recollection; the blind spot was too great.

It wasn't easy, though, to pigeonhole my father, particularly when I thought about how I had gotten the help I needed when I hit bottom in the spring of 2008. Once my brother told my father that my need was extreme, he gave the money on the spot, no questions. In fact, his unhesitating response was, "That's what money is for." At the time, my father was eighty-seven years old, already in declining health and suffering from some dementia, and he surely did not comprehend anything about what was happening to me. Nevertheless, he didn't ask questions, he just provided the money, big money. So while he had not given me some things that I needed, he had given me others, and I was left with conflicting feelings about him that in their own way were as intense as those I felt for my mother.

CHAPTER SIXTEEN

CAMO

I WAS SET UP FROM YOUTH to trip and fall over life's trials, because, having been taught nothing and exposed to almost nothing "real," (all of my family's messiness having been swept carefully under the carpet), I knew nothing about how to handle things. I studied people for years, figuring out what behavior to mimic, how to react to a given situation. I used to say that I took a lot of my cues on mothering from Leo, who I joked with some truth was a better mother than I was. This may not have been one hundred percent true, but he did exhibit more of the typical maternal instinct than I. After I gave birth to our first child, he took great pleasure in cleaning up the meconium, the viscous black poop that babies excrete for the first couple of days. Need I say more? He was not the extreme, though—I once actually met a woman who exhibited pride in her child's Apgar score, the post-birth measurement of respiration, heart rate and other physical responses. She got competitive about it, asked me what my son, David's, had been. David was four at the time, and I didn't recollect anything about his score, if indeed I had ever known it.

After David's birth, I remember being devastated that I didn't have that instantaneous connection with my son that I'd been led to believe came with the territory if you were female and breathing. I surreptitiously watched other people for cues on how to act: the baby nurse who came for two weeks, my mother-in-law, the mailman, anyone who seemed to know how to talk to and care for a baby. I was scared, oh how I was scared. It was dawning on me that it had been one thing to leverage myself into life by getting married, but it was an altogether different thing to do it with a baby. My fantasy of creating a circle of warmth and love of likeminded individuals who just happened to be my children was on life support and I had no idea what to do. I don't know how I got through those first three months, but I did, and at exactly three months, the magic happened and I connected to my son. I was giving him a bath in the sink, and I noticed that I was no longer terrified that I would drop him, and what I was doing felt completely natural. I basked in the glow of that feeling for all of an hour, and then plunged into ambivalence: "I'm too comfortable with this, it's too seductive. I'd better go back to work right now, because if I don't, I never will." I wonder what my life would have been if I had given in to the seduction.

Bonding in three months was a big improvement over the previous generation's track record in my family. When David was a few months old I took him to The Factory, as the locus of the family business was known. My father took him out on the floor of the plant and held him up like Simba in *The Lion King*. One of the employees came up and started talking about how he had felt holding his own son, to which my father responded, "I don't know, I didn't hold my own children until they were two." The guy, an average Joe, looked at my father like he had three heads, but that's the way it had been in a very narrow swath of society during my parents' generation. My brother was raised by a nurse who made him eat soap when he misbehaved. I got lucky, having been raised from birth by Amelia and George, only trotted out for cameo appearances until I was four and my mother decided to go hands on, after being roundly criticized by her own mother for dereliction of duty based on my failure to identify colors. Amelia and George were loving to me, and in many ways I was content as a little kid, squishing around barefoot in the mud and going with them and Pamela to services at their church. I remember the prayer fans waving and "Amen Jesus" echoing in the summer heat. I still love gospel music in a way that I suspect few white people can.

As a parent, I am all about the psychology of it, not the regular mom stuff: I want my kids to know what makes them tick, how to be in relationships, to recognize the value of truth and the inutility of secrets, and to find work where their passions lie. I would also throw all of that away for them to be happy at least most of the time, as they seem to be. Good, I like to see vertical progress in families.

This question of authenticity has bedeviled me my whole life. I had a strange role model in my mother, who grew up in Brooklyn but by the time I knew her called a tomato a "tomahto" and God help the butler if he didn't serve from the left. I mentioned this to a cousin. It turns out that her own mother, my aunt, presumably also from a middle-class background, had created a new father out of whole cloth, Count von Valt (pronounced "Vahlt"), who, according to the story, had heroically returned to Europe to free his family domain from the Nazis. No wonder the Baby Boomers, at least those who are not too distant from the immigrants in their background, need psychiatrists.

My New York cousin didn't believe a word of what her mother told her, while I bought all of what was being sold to me. That wasn't new: my yearning to be city smart and outspoken like people from the North and my fear of the ramifications started early. When I was in ninth grade, I became friends with a Northern girl who had just moved to town. When she would come to my house to sleep over, Southern hospitality dictated that I cede the prime spot at the head of the bed to her, so she could lean back in comfort while we rehashed the latest school dramas. I was puzzled and a little bemused when I went over to her house and we settled in to chat, me at the foot of the bed, propped up awkwardly on my elbow, she reclining against her pillows. Where was my turn at the helm? Southern courtesy required that I keep my mouth shut, which I did, and register my complaint internally, if at all.

Authenticity gets complicated when you take someone like me and throw her into a family like mine. I was born with a tendency toward self-examination and an inclination away from the mainstream, not so much attracted to or proficient in logic, manipulation, money sense or physical beauty (a big focus of my parents). The choice to be different being unavailable, I carefully tucked myself away, way away, and built a precarious scaffold with the tools at my disposal: a good brain, a good eye for aesthetics, a dry sense of humor and the ability to fake the appearance of fitting in. The downside was that I had to learn to live from the outside in instead of the inside out, scrambling to interpret signals so subtle that they held little meaning in order to respond in ways that would at least approximate what my family and polite society would expect. And I learned to wear a mask—I was the original Wizard of Oz, the real action all took place behind the curtain.

Once I got out of my parents' house and went to college I should have been a hippie, I really should have, it's just that I didn't find them all that authentic either. Like every other group I've ever been around, there was the regular cast of characters: arrivistes, wannabees, hangers on, the real deal, and the shameless self-promoters. The pretty girls still got the guys more often than not, and pretty still meant the same thing that it meant in "straight" people—good body, sexy, outgoing, self-confident, good sense of humor. If you think that shit was true about "looks don't matter, everything is peace and love, everybody loves everybody," it wasn't. Good looks just got re-defined and bathing became less de rigueur; a little dirt was even considered attractive. I thought so myself.

I later learned the real reason why the Divine One, Blessed Be He, preserved me from becoming a hippie. In my dotage I became a sort of Guns N' Roses groupie, attending three of their 2011-2012 concerts in the space of twelve weeks. Because of my love of their early music, I started reading books about the original group and its members, one of them being Slash's autobiography. One quote from his book resonated particularly strongly with me:

> It's tough to be the kind of person who hangs around the fringier edges of society if you're not a musician or someone who has a purpose being there. Everyone else is a disposable player out there in the void on the scene. Most of the girls who dated us back then were these innocent chicks whose lives were changed forever after one of us came into it for however long it lasted. We were like a vacuum back then that sucked people up and spit them out; a ton of people around us fell by the wayside that way. Some people died, not because of anything we did to them, but as a side effect of being too close to the flame. People would get attracted to our fucked-up weird life and just get it wrong and drown in our riptide.[3]

While he was describing the 1980s, I don't think it would have been much different in the '60s and '70s. I had not a shred of doubt that I would have been exactly that kind of chick and would have suffered exactly the fate described. Just think of a blonde-haired moth with a slight double chin and an earnest look in her eyes—that would have been me, careening towards the flame at breakneck speed. Somewhere inside I knew how vulnerable I was and that for me it wouldn't have been a stubbed toe, it would have been closer to decapitation to get involved in the scene that attracted me so mightily, so I stayed away and watched enviously from the fringes.

CHAPTER SEVENTEEN

☙

ARCHAEOLOGY, ART, AND
ADVENTURE

ESPITE MY TENDENCY to watch life from
the sidelines, I had a fun-loving, imaginative
side that propelled me through some wonderful
times and great adventures. I started out as an
anthropology major in college, even went on a
dig the summer after my freshman year. Six of
us, indentured to two handsome young graduate
students working on their theses, roomed in a small
flat in Sheffield, England, leaving bright and early
every morning to drive out to the moors between

Sheffield and Manchester and launch ourselves at the smelly peat, digging away like a bunch of misplaced prairie dogs.

I spent most days bundled under layers of sweaters (1972 was a summer of record cold in England), monotonously scraping my trowel across the peat and sucking the mud from pieces of flint and chert (black quartz) to look for 10,000-year-old markings. You got used to the taste after a while, and sucking the mud off saved the effort of washing all the little bits. I once found a small trove of flint tools, but it took so long to reveal them by methodical excavation that I lost interest before they had fully appeared.

At night though, things got more interesting. Somewhere along the line our living arrangements turned communal, down to casual nakedness and shared beds. I was too shy to participate fully, but became quite used to naked guys wandering in and out of the bathroom while I was in the tub and thought nothing of it. I still remember that summer fondly as my own slightly belated "Summer of Love," Suzy Marmalade coming into her own, if only for a little while.

I went back to school in the fall, and Rex, one of the grad students, asked if I had any friends with whom to fix him up. I trotted out my roommate of the previous year, the one person whose outlook was, if anything, more clueless than mine, and promised him a good time. I don't know what I was thinking, but a good time was not how either of them described it. I tried again, with a sexy, sophisticated friend, but cautioned Rex that he probably wasn't going to like her. Two days later they moved in together, proving that I didn't know any more about men back then than I do now.

I was always a crammer at school, and one night I stayed up all night at my friend Harold's house writing a paper. It was the one time I took real amphetamines (as opposed to diet pills, which I ate like candy), and I was still speeding when I finished the paper at 6:00 a.m. Harold was asleep, I was excited, so I got in my car and drove over to Rex's house. The front door was unlocked and I pushed through the screen door and barged in, yelling "Hey, guess what. . .?" only to stop in my tracks at the sight of Rex materializing in front of me, buck naked with a shotgun pointed at my midsection. A loaded shotgun, with the safety off. I learned my lesson, never surprised anybody like that again.

I went back to Harold's, hung out for a while and, in an effort to recover from my earlier shock, watched him paint. Harold was a superb artist and a good friend; he often asked if he could paint my portrait, but I always said, "Not now, wait until I lose some weight." I never did and he never did, and after he visited me once in Atlanta after college, we fell out of touch.

Years later, attending an opening in Norfolk honoring artists whose works had recently been added to the Chrysler Museum of Art's contemporary collection, I ran into Harold. I didn't recognize him at first; he had created an Elton John-esque persona that was hard to see around, but I finally went up and asked and it was indeed Harold. We went to dinner and caught up. I mentioned all the times that he had asked to do my portrait and I had refused. Harold said, 'You should have done it, I just painted Donald Trump's last week." He wasn't kidding; I later visited him in his loft in Chelsea and he showed me walls of photographs taken of him with celebrities.

Damn.

To balance the scales, though, I owned a painting at the time that I ran into Harold, which, unbeknownst to me, would later prove to be my own personal lottery ticket. Soon after I moved to Hong Kong in 1994, I heard about a contemporary art fair, on the order of Art Basel or the Armory Show in New York. I went, armed with little or no information about contemporary art in Asia, but keen to look and keener to buy, not for a great sum, just something.

I walked the fair, walked it again, and came to rest at the booth of a well-known Hong Kong dealer, the top dealer in the city for contemporary art. I liked what he was showing, but something pushed me to ask if he had anything stashed away that wasn't on show. The dealer, Chunn, said yes, and opened a closet door, allowing me to browse through some paintings stacked against the wall. I found one that I liked very much, the face of a man with kinky hair, ostensibly a villager from someplace up in the mountains of Tibet. Chunn showed me a large coffee table art book about contemporary Chinese art in which the piece appeared with some commentary about the artist. That clinched it for me. I bought the piece for $3,500 (U.S. dollars), which to me at the time was not a great expenditure for art. I had come into some money a few years earlier and had quickly become accustomed to spending what many people would consider large sums on art and jewelry. Chunn gave me the book with the painting in it as a gift, so I went home happy.

The painting hung on the walls of my homes in Hong Kong, Atlanta and Norfolk, both pre- and post-divorce. Then there came a time, post-divorce, when I couldn't pay my rent. I was struggling with depression, out of a job, and thinking that I had no prospects of finding one. That was close to the truth: there were not many legal jobs available to me, not being licensed in Virginia. As it turned out, I ultimately got one of the very few positions for which I was eligible.

I called a friend who was a local estate seller of great repute and asked for help selling whatever I had that might bring in a meaningful sum of money. Among other things, she researched the painting of the Tibetan villager and came back with astonishing news. The artist had become popular in recent years for painting and sculpting green dogs; over and over, nothing but green dogs. "Fine with me," I said, "so, what's the bottom line?" "If it sells at all, your painting should go for $60,000." Shades of *Antiques Roadshow,* I nearly fell over.

I told her to go ahead and put the piece up for sale with the online auction service she favored. It was a week-long auction, and nothing happened for the first six days, twenty-three hours and fifty minutes. Finally, with ten minutes to go, the magic number "1" appeared next to the piece in the column headed "number of bids," and that is how the auction ended, one bid for $60,000. It was probably a great investment on some savvy art collector's part, but I was beyond caring about that. I now had some cash at my disposal, a minor miracle, plus it was an amazing rush, one I hope to replicate some day.

I have always had a passion for art and jewelry—collecting, not creating. When my parents asked me what I wanted for my twenty-fifth birthday, I said "collectible art." They came back from their next trip to England with my present, a sketch and a lithograph by Henry Moore, and, as a collector, as long as the money held out, I never looked back.

Unfortunately, I missed my footing on the equally obvious career path. Sotheby's, the famous auction house, offered an internship in London, and that's what I should have pursued after college instead of law. Ironically, when I moved to New York in 1985 after leaving my Atlanta law firm, midway into my year as a minimum wage employee at a Soho art gallery, I spotted an ad for an in-house attorney position at Sotheby's. I applied and was called in for an interview, but the discussions stopped when I decided that I didn't want to work full time. Probably a good thing, since the company's lawyer almost went to jail for assisting in illegal practices in 2000. That could have been me; glad it wasn't.

So I stayed in my minimum wage job at the gallery in Soho. While it didn't do much for paying the bills, it was a fine education of a particular kind, because this was not the Rolls-Royce of galleries in New York—quite the contrary. The other salesgirls were more like hookers; I can still see one of them, a young, nubile girl, hoisting herself up on the reception desk, smoothing down her mini-skirt and crossing her legs, directing the attention of her potential client, a man in a full length raccoon coat, to the most expensive piece in the gallery. The fight for commissions was hair-raising, and I lasted all of three days on the sales floor before being gratefully banished to the basement to take on the job of entering the inventory by hand in bound volumes.

I became friendly with the guy who hung the shows and did the heavy work around the gallery. One night I walked with him through Tompkins

Square Park, littered with used needles, over to a bar on Avenue A. They were showing Divine in the film *Pink Flamingos,* there was performance art going on (fun in theory but boring in practice) and I was as happy as a pig in shit. The only thing that made me happier was when we walked over to Avenue B, and from there my friend pointed to the rest of Alphabet City, where it was too dangerous to go. One of my tastes of life on the edge, God how I loved it.

CHAPTER EIGHTEEN

MONEY, MAKEUP, MUSIC, AND MADNESS

PINK FLOYD GOT IT RIGHT: money is a gas. Or at least, it has been in my life. I started out at the top and slowly wended my way down, the exact inverse of the American Dream. As a child I lived in the place that I have described—one of the biggest, baddest houses in Atlanta, acres of land within the city limits, and a house that looked like something lifted out of *Gone with the Wind*. Other people thought we were stratospherically wealthy. I knew this because their kids would say it to me out loud as a matter of course, and I took it for the truth. It seemed plausible to my young eyes, what with dinner served on silver platters by a butler in a white coat, a laundress who lived in a log cabin on the property, and the acres of gardens and crops tended by various and sundry drunks and half-wits whom my mother hired from the local street corner. (My mother was a CEO manqué and spent the bulk of her life managing her motley crew of servants with an iron hand, issuing edicts about the condition of the riding mower like it affected the state of the nation.)

I felt like an heiress apparent, and part of the message, overtly, was that spending money with abandon was a God-given right. When I was fifteen years old I had bespoke leather riding boots made for me in England by Maxwell of London, bootmaker since 1750. I lived in Paris for a year in college and any time I needed cash I would go to my father's business associate at 20 rue Tronchet, behind La Madeleine, and pick up a bag of French francs. I mean a bag, made of paper, with piles of notes swirling around in the bottom. I traveled with my parents off and on until I was married at thirty-one, and we navigated through Western Europe like minor royalty. Leo once showed me a magazine article naming the top twenty restaurants in the world. I had eaten at ten of them by the time I was thirty.

The family trips to Europe were the best of times. The tension between my mother and me abated, and the three of us (my brother didn't come after the early trips) took great pleasure in the food, the shopping, the sights and the adventure, above all the adventure. I must have gotten my delight in the unusual from my mother, and in Europe we found communion on this point, always on the lookout for some new and surprising tableau to point out to the other.

My mother also took our time in Europe as an opportunity to teach me the finer points of life, as in 1968 at age fifteen when I found myself with her in the offices of M. Pierre Arpels at Van Cleef & Arpels on the Place Vendôme in Paris. Here I learned how to negotiate for fine jewelry, the technique being that even a lady asked once, but only once, "Is this your best price?" to which the vendor knew that he must respond by coming down anywhere from 10 to 20% on the piece, depending on its value. The lady must know not to ask for a discount on items below a certain value, at the time about $2,000; that was considered gauche, since items in that price range were on the order of costume jewelry, and if you needed to ask for a discount on that, you were in the wrong place.

When I graduated from law school at age twenty-eight, a friend and I took the Pan Am tour around the world. As long as you kept flying in the same direction, it was a flat fare, $1,700, for unlimited stops. We went to London, Dijon, Paris, Metz (east of Paris, I had a friend there), Cannes, Vienna, Bangkok, Singapore, Hong Kong, a side trip to China, Tokyo, Kyoto, Mt. Fuji, Hawaii, San Francisco and New York. We stayed in top hotels and were treated royally by my father's business associates—picked up by cars and drivers, given access to local silk shops in Bangkok and off-the-beaten-track kimono shops in Tokyo, and served fabulous meals wherever we went.

A few years later, I went back to Europe on my own, making my way through London and Copenhagen before meeting up with my parents in Venice. I sometimes think that it was a good thing that I went on and spent money that might better have been saved, because I got to see and do things that would have been lost to me forever. On this trip, on a whim, I took the Concorde back from London to New York, conversing in French with an Ethiopian man as we broke the sound barrier. Was it worth it? No question.

From this background I grew into a kind of casual prima donna, aloof, entitled, but not overly demanding or intimidating. My saving graces were that I had a dry wit, didn't take myself seriously and had a way of making the truth into a torpedo, vastly appealing to some people. I was so openly cavalier about money that I earned a bye on it—it was universally agreed that my sense of entitlement was laced with enough irreverence to make it forgivable.

The upswing of my life as an heiress culminated with a nice-sized inheritance in 1987. It wasn't enough for Leo and me to buy a McMansion, but sufficient to launch me into a retail business that would surround me with the glamour I thought was my due. I hired a consultant and traveled to London, Paris, Milan and Florence, scouring the luxury gift fairs for unique and stylish objects and porcelain not otherwise seen in Atlanta (in some cases not seen elsewhere in the United States). I reveled in the glamour and the fun for four years, until in 1994 Leo, David, Juliana and I moved to Hong Kong for Leo's job. By 1996, that was the end of the store and my investment— as everyone had warned me before I left for Hong Kong, it turned out to be impossible to run a small, independent store from thousands of miles away. However, I counted myself lucky that although I ended up with no cash and everything gone, I also ended up with no debts and, remarkably, a good name which still gets favorable recognition many years later.

Through the Hong Kong years I still had money and made enough extra to continue to live lavishly enough. It is Hong Kong in a nutshell that I, an American, made money selling Vietnamese chopsticks designed in Hanoi by a Frenchwoman to an old-line British department store whose principal customers were Chinese. We lived in Stanley on the

South side of Hong Kong Island, with one, then two, Filipina housekeepers, the second devoted exclusively to Rachel, who was born there in 1996.

In 1998, tired of being expatriates and wanting to raise our children around family, we moved back to Atlanta. It was there that the coup de grâce to my lifestyle was administered by the internet stock boom. I bought what was being sold, hook, line and sinker. The new era bullshit fed right into my desire to be as wealthy as my parents, not tomorrow but yesterday. I had waited long enough on the fringes; I don't think anything could have stopped me from investing in those soaring stocks. Like most people, I had enough success to get intoxicated and stay that way until getting sober was no longer a possibility, not voluntarily and not until it was way too late.

And like many people who participated in that particular market frenzy, the bloodletting for me was severe, about a 70% loss. Not too long thereafter I proceeded to get divorced, and the subsequent descent to my personal financial bottom was swift and merciless. I seriously contemplated what I would do when all of the money was gone, and whether my daughter, Rachel, could realistically be expected to come stay with me in a trailer during the weeks that I had custody. It never came to that, but by June of 2010, I was living in a tiny apartment with a washer/dryer room in the parking lot and gaping cracks around the doors and windows through which the frigid wind blew in winter. I was jobless, not by design, and close to being broke. I was not cool with this by any means, but I was trying to tolerate the idea that I was put here to learn something and that this was part of the lesson. Who knows, maybe I was going to make a career out of teaching formerly rich people how to be poor with grace.

The part of me that was not cool with being poor insisted on equal time. My God, I had had to give up my Laura Mercier makeup in favor of drug store imitations; where would the insults end? Giving it up was a painful moment, for makeup held high symbolism for me. When I was in eleventh grade I flirted with anorexia, got so thin that my ribs stuck out. It was the first time I could prop my knees up on the back of the chair in front of me at school and see a space between my thighs. I began dating a fraternity boy at Emory and started having the semblance of a normal teenage life. I was so pleased one day when I saw my ribs as I postured naked in front of my mirror that I marched into my mother's room to show her. She pitched a fit about how vain I was, and how I needed to be taught a lesson: no more makeup for me. I was devastated; the spark went out and I set about bringing down my fragile house of cards—purposely got fat, stopped dating, retreated from life. Thinking back on it, it seems like an overreaction on my part, but that was the dynamic of the day.

I think that I bought makeup after that, but I did not learn how to use it and really don't remember wearing it much until eleven years later, when a friend marched me into Bergdorf Goodman's, up to the makeup counter, and ordered $200 worth of Marcella Borghese products for me (I paid), including strict instructions on how to use them. This was the same friend with whom I traveled around the world; in fact, Bergdorf's was our last stop on that trip. I have been forever grateful to her for giving me back a sense of femininity.

The makeup incident with my mother was not the only time I took discouragement and ran with it. I always thought I'd be a writer, that English was the path for me, until I had Mrs. Kellogg as a teacher in eleventh grade. (Clearly, eleventh grade was a turning point in my life; unfortunately, I missed the turn.) We had been studying symbolism and one day she gave a test on our abilities to identify it. At the end of the test, she posed the question, "Did you prevail or merely survive?" I confidently checked "prevail," and was bowled over when I got a D back on the test. Apparently, I had missed the point of everything.

It didn't take much to knock me down for the count. I did not willingly take another English class for the rest of my life. For the one English course I had to take in college I picked "Eighteenth-Century Novel," each tome more painful than the last; I must have been punishing myself. I hope I never see the name "Tobias Smollett" in print again. I wrote a single page of a children's book after the birth of my first child in 1988, and after that, unless you count legal contracts, not another word until I started this book twenty-two years later.

I did the same thing with music. My college roommate has often reminded me that when she and her parents walked into our dorm room for the first time, I was sitting on my bed cross legged listening to Blood Rock, a 1970s hard rock band whose claim to fame was a song called DOA with explicit lyrics about people dying in a plane crash. In the same vein, I was the only one in my conservative circle at college who liked Black Sabbath and Frank Zappa and experimented with people like Coltrane and Miles Davis. (I couldn't stand *Bitches Brew*—I threw the album out, which I know will be sacrilege to some).

Once I got out of college in 1975, though, it's like somebody turned off a tap, and I quit listening to new kinds of music, went completely mainstream, and it wasn't until some time after 2000 that I rediscovered my love of electric guitar. Google, YouTube and iTunes have restored my music to me, and I spend hours researching "100 best guitar solos" and "sounds like Steve Vai." I am a huge fan of blues rock, love "Tied to the Whipping Post," "Loan me a Dime" (Duane Allman solo), and am discovering Kenny Wayne Shepherd and, decades after the fact, Stevie Ray Vaughan, so that makes me happy.

How do you cut off parts of yourself so completely, not for days or weeks, but for decades? Sometimes I felt like a schizophrenic, multiple personalities raging about inside of me, all but one carefully locked up. I feared the madness that this implied, and was always very careful to protect myself from it, lest I descend into it and never come back.

Why is it always "descend?" Do people think it is like going down a staircase, with your long gown draped over one arm, toe heel placed after toe heel carefully on the steps so there is no misstep? I guarantee that madness is not like that. It is like opening a bottle of ketchup and tilting it up, thinking that just a little is going to come out, but by accident the bottle is at the wrong angle and the tomato sauce just pours and pours, and there all of your French fries sit, soggy, inedible, ruined.

I once went to a meeting of a group called Recovery Inc. I think of them as the Stepford Wives of the mental health recovery world, with their stock phrases that they solemnly parrot in response to a member's story. One of those phrases is "Nervous people feel longer and stronger." I detested the phrase when I heard it, and it was all I could do to keep to my chair and not bolt out of the door. The statement is wrong on so many levels, but it is right in the sense that there is a "more, more, more" quality to madness.

About the same time as my Recovery Inc. experience I read a memoir by a young man, a singer, who drank and drugged his way through twenty years of his life. He was literally drunk, stoned, and high on cocaine every single day and night ("gack," he called it, funny to me, I'd never heard that word before). I can tell you that whatever his problem was, it was not a predisposition to madness. I would be so long locked up if I had done for a month what he did for two decades.

The first time I tried marijuana it scared me out of my wits. I am not a person who remembers much of my life in vivid detail, but I remember where I was sitting (on the Brown Jordan webbed rocking chair outside of my parents' pool house), who I was with (Carlton Smith), the time of day (a hot summer night at about 11:00 p.m.) and, in spades, how I felt, the first time I got stoned. Really scared was how I felt. The part of me that was behind the wheel didn't take kindly to me deliberately driving downhill with the brakes out, and kept saying, "Watch out, you might go away and never come back!"

I thought that was a real possibility, and as a result, while I finally got accustomed to pot and got high regularly in college, I stayed far away from psychedelic drugs, never tried acid or mushrooms or anything like that. They beckoned me, they really did; it would have been a big relief to trade in misery at worst and low-grade anxiety at best for a good old-fashioned hallucination every once in a while, but I just didn't trust my mind to do the right thing and make its way home at the end of the trip. Since I gave up pot after college (other than the one trip to Amsterdam), I had to wait until I was much older for a really good chemically-induced high. That came as a welcome byproduct of my triennial colonoscopy—Versed coursing through my veins, absolute heaven for three glorious minutes.

As of my last colonoscopy, they don't use Versed anymore, favoring instead some drug that puts you out instantaneously. When the anesthesiologist told me, I felt like a child whose favorite toy had been thrown out and I actually made him go look for some Versed. It was a huge disappointment that he came back empty handed. This may sound like a joke, but if you have gone through years of feeling like shit 50% of the time and at some level unnerved the other 50% of the time, a few of minutes of legal carefree bliss was like a gift from the gods.

CHAPTER NINETEEN

HONEYMOON'S END

I HAVE ALWAYS ENJOYED LIVING in big cities—
Atlanta, Paris, Miami, New York and Hong Kong.
I am a city girl through and through, and while I
lived for a time in the suburbs when my children
were young, I never felt alive there like I did in
the city. Just the same, I was the one who largely
engineered my family's move to Norfolk, Virginia
in 2001, although we could have moved anywhere
in the world. At the time I wanted to get some
distance from my parents, and it was my opinion
that, being in our late forties with three youngish

children, if we were going to move away from "my people," it only made sense to move towards Leo's. Norfolk was his home town and most of his family was still there. After fifteen years of marriage, they were my family, too, so that seemed reason enough to move there. I think it made the place feel safe, or at least safer than I felt living in the same town as my own family, and that must have been what I was looking for. When all was said and done, living in Norfolk did not turn out to be safe for me at all, but I couldn't have known that in the beginning.

After we moved to Norfolk, there was a honeymoon period, which lasted three months. I was thrilled with the diners and the greasy spoons and decided that there was great edge to be found here, over by the Chesapeake Bay where the houses were being reclaimed from the prostitutes and the sailors who pissed openly in the yards, down in the honky-tonk parts of the Virginia Beach strip, with motels in neon and pastel and kids with long hair and skateboards. The problem was, I didn't belong in those places and I hated the places I did belong. The first time somebody asked me if I would join their group to make fruit baskets for a local charity, I reacted like I'd been snakebit. It went downhill from there.

I tried to fit in, I really did. I worked at the gift shop at the Chrysler Museum of Art and joined the contemporary art group there. A couple of years later I bought a horse and threw myself back into riding, the sport of my youth. I worked at dreary law jobs, as shop girl in a design space, and as an administrative assistant at a mortgage company. (If you think the impending housing market crisis was a secret, think again). I took up yoga. I started a vintage handbag business in an antiques co-op and then online. (I must say, the website was magnificent.) I did mom things, though I never threw myself into my children's school activities like some women. I used to call myself the "anti-mom" as far as that went—I was allergic to streamers; they had the same effect on me as fruit baskets.

For the first three years in Norfolk, I was like some civilizations you hear about: they hit a high point, then decline until a new emperor comes on the scene, someone with lots of energy and enthusiasm. Then they rise again until he gets poisoned or the momentum stops, then it's back to the Dark Ages until the next Justinian comes along. Each new job, each new endeavor, was like the bold new emperor, always followed by the decline. Then, at the beginning of my fourth year in Norfolk, came the Bubonic Plague. All the lights went out; I mean all.

My marriage had started coming undone some time before, but I deliberately overlooked it. Divorce wasn't in my playbook, not even in the appendix. But the dynamic got uglier and uglier, and I was hitting lower and lower bottoms, until there really wasn't much choice in the matter, not if I wanted to keep functioning.

Leo and I had become best friends after meeting during our first year of law school and we married eight years later on the strength of that friendship. I used to say that we were "madly in like," and we really were; we adored each other. I thought that there were far worse foundations on which to base a lifelong commitment. We started out as a modern couple, equal in earning power and equal in most everything. We complemented each other's shortcomings—I was a fast decision maker, he was cautious. He was terrifically outgoing, I was a little introverted. We both loved art and travel and considered ourselves sophisticates. The fact that our marriage came apart is testimony to how complicated the recipe for a successful marriage is, and how hard it really is to know in advance how you will weather the storms, particularly if your bond has never been tested. Ours had not been, but as our marriage wore on, it was tested, severely.

I have not talked much about myself as an addict. I had an eating disorder for most of my life (thankfully in abeyance for some time), not anorexia or bulimia like you hear about these days, but good old fashioned bingeing and starving. I don't think people understand anymore what that disorder really is; I certainly haven't read or heard much about it in ages. It was not pretty—it was hiding in a locked bathroom so that Leo and the children didn't see me stuffing cake down my throat compulsively, sometimes choking because I couldn't take the time to swallow completely; the compulsion was so great to keep going, not to stop until I passed out like a drunk. It was spending a lot of money setting up my food stash and making sure there was a time that I could find isolation to eat it without Leo's sneers to upset me or his cajolements to interfere with my mission, which I had planned with military precision. It was the dizziness and nausea that came from not eating for three days in a row. It was the high of the fix as the sugar sang through my veins, and the pleasure of giving in, not fighting anymore, taking over my mind. It was the crash when the sugar in my bloodstream plummeted, my eyelids drooped and my energy was sapped and I hated myself for hurting myself and my family and being helpless to do anything about it. The bingeing part is more than anything else a primal experience; there is very little thought to it, and for someone like me who felt varying degrees of alienation and marginalization for most of my life, it sometimes even had an element of purpose and aliveness to it.

Leo watched me cycle through relatively mild episodes of bingeing and depression followed by speedy recoveries during the early years of our marriage. Then it got worse, and the cycles lasted longer, until finally in 2000 I checked into that first program at the eating disorders clinic. Leo came to a couple of meetings there, but he did not understand any part of the lingo or the dynamics or what role he might play, and to me it felt like he did not want to help me. For a long time I held that against him. He in turn held my disease and the burden it placed on the family against me. And it *was* a burden—the addiction led me to depression, which led to more bingeing which led to more depression. It was a hard cycle to break and a hard cycle to watch, and it is nobody's fault that the marriage did not survive its sporadic appearance in our lives, unpredictable in its swift descent and just as unpredictable in its departure, returning me to my sunny, relatively unencumbered disposition, plus whatever pounds I had gained. Add in the other assorted baggage that Leo and I each carried around, and we didn't have much of a chance.

We were married for nineteen years, many of them good, many of them filled with laughter and sharing and intimacy. Those times grew less and less, and the bad feelings and shouting matches took over, until for me it was either leave under my own steam or in a strait jacket.

I have often been thought to act impulsively, but it was only true some of the time. The rest of the time, it was as if there was an invisible cylinder inside of me, and inside that cylinder there was a part of me that was working away at whatever problem was troubling me. As the work progressed, the cylinder filled up, and when it was full to the brim, it crested like an overfull glass, then spilled its contents into my awareness. When that happened, not only did I instantly know the answer, I knew the problem and everything in between. I also knew what had to be done, but when I did it, I seemed impulsive, because no one was privy to the underlying process, least of all me.

That was how my marriage ended. One morning Leo woke me up out of a sound sleep to start the day with an argument and the water hit the brim, bubbled over and cascaded down the sides in one smooth sequence. I knew I was done. Though it was only weeks later that I served him with papers and moved out into an apartment that, on my lawyer's advice, I had secretly rented and furnished in the interim, this was no sudden impulse. It was the fruit of thousands of hours of internal combustion, my little engine chugging away over the conflict I was feeling.

I said to myself: "Stay? I feel bad, real bad. Can it change? Can things go back to the way they were?" I thought back to a moment in the wee hours one night before we were married when I looked at my whirling dervish husband-to-be, for once relaxed, his head tilted back on the sofa, eyes half closed. There was a subtler than usual quality to his energy but the charm was still there, and I remembered the powerful attraction that I had felt for that person. I married him partly on the strength of that moment, thinking that if he could be that way once he could be that way again, maybe stay that way. I had a habit of getting caught by the moments and ignoring the hours, days, weeks, months and years. My divorce was a bid to break that habit, to learn to bet with the odds.

Okay, so the answer was to go. Where would I go? I was afraid to be alone, and this was not my town, I had no people there. What about the kids? How would I tell them?

The children came with me for two weeks, which secured my custody rights, and then we settled into a routine of visitation. Things went along okay for a couple of months. I immediately got a gerbil, Roxy, for Rachel; this had been a condition of her coming with me at the outset. The dog ate Roxy (sad looking thing, a chewed up gerbil, if you've never seen one), and I replaced it with another named Rocky. Same result. Rocky's death was traumatic for all of us; he actually had personality, was chock full of it. I checked all of the local pet stores and managed to replace Rocky with two new gerbils before Rachel got home from school, so we got over that hump with relative ease. Horace the kitten also joined our family about this time.

Pretty quickly, though, reality hit me. There I was, in a town where all of my friends were my ex-husband's friends, all my family his family; there was no city as such to offer me diversity in numbers or entertainment, and I had a job that I hated (mortgage subservicing regulation, a dazzling if little known area of legal practice). Leo and I were in the financial settlement part of the divorce, and anyone who has been through a divorce will tell you that that's where the shit really hits the fan. I would receive scathing emails from Leo (in those days he was at least my mother's equal in the anger department), open them and read them as fast as I could, through slitted eyes like I was watching a scary movie. I closed the emails when I couldn't stand it anymore and opened them again two or three days later, when the fear had subsided and I could try to formulate a response. This went on for months, since we tried to negotiate directly rather than through our lawyers, in order to save money on legal fees. A real set up for a case of the vapors. Anyone with any sense would have seen my downfall coming a mile away. I wish I could say that I followed the mature, adult path for handling the divorce and its fallout, but it wasn't quite like that. Instead, I gave up and turned the reins over to Suzy Marmalade, the child who had never grown up. She took me on quite a roller coaster ride in search of ways to get through the tumult.

PART THREE

THE QUEST

CHAPTER TWENTY

WHAT'S WRONG WITH SUZY?

T HE SEARCH FOR PEACE following the implosion of my marriage was not the beginning of my quest, not by a long shot. I had been searching for ways to help myself for years. Progress, however, was elusive, because for the longest time I was completely ignorant about what was wrong with me, although I was aware that I had felt a strong sense of malaise for as long as I could remember. The first time I registered it I was in second grade, going through the lunch line. I took two extra cups of ice cream (remember the small cups with the pull-tab lids and the wooden paddle spoons?) and hid them in my underwear. I didn't feel safe without them, like a squirrel hiding nuts against a bleak winter to come.

This was also the first public manifestation of my food addiction, and it had embarrassing results. After I left the cafeteria, I forgot all about the two ice cream cups snugly tucked in my underpants. It was Christmastime, and my class was busy decorating our tree. I was standing on a chair hanging ornaments and I noticed a boy pointing in my direction. Then he yelled, "What's that?" I looked down and saw white rivulets of melted vanilla ice cream streaming down my legs. I hopped off the chair and sprinted to the bathroom, humiliated and in tears. I washed my legs off and cleaned my petticoat, which was sticky with ice cream. I don't think I ever told anyone what had happened, and no one asked me. The look on my face must have been enough to stop the questions.

Growing up, I paid attention to my issues only if they were causing problems in my life. As the years went by, they did, and I experimented widely, hoping to find something that would bring me peace from the moments of crisis that cycled faster and faster the older I got. For twenty-nine years I slogged through therapists in the double digits, not to mention three hospitalizations. I heard a lot of things that sounded like answers—"you suffer from depression," "you suffer from anxiety," "you suffer from mood swings," "you suffer from fragile self-esteem." I was also advised after my discharge from Alexander that I was a traveler through the Dark Night of the Soul. This refers to the painful journey out of ego and into awareness and harmony described by Saint John of the Cross, a sixteenth-century mystic. Very cool. I couldn't wait to get there.

On the technical, DSM-IV side (DSM-IV is the psychiatric profession's diagnostic manual), the confusion was equally great. In 2008, when I was an inpatient at Farraday, the experts diagnosed me with non-specific bipolar disorder, not to mention complex post-traumatic stress disorder, panic disorder and binge eating disorder. Farraday was private pay, so there was no incentive to find a label just to satisfy an insurance company. One and a half years later, again an inpatient, this time at Alexander, my attending physician diagnosed me with bipolar II disorder, not to be confused with non-specific bipolar. Two weeks after I was discharged from Alexander, Dr. Renway, the psychiatrist who put me there in the first place, opined that I did not have bipolar disorder of any variety, in fact no diagnosable disorder at all, merely "affective surges/storms, difficulty regulating feelings, discreet episodes not rising to the level of major depressive disorder." To round things out, two months later I was accepted into a clinical trial for people with treatment resistant depression.

I had the unpleasant sensation that no one knew what to do with me. Even my nice young therapist showed up one day with a pamphlet for another private pay inpatient clinic, although she assured me that she could "handle me" alone and this was just in response to a question I had asked about treatment options. I believed her, sort of.

I had gotten into a lot of trouble in my years of treatment believing that my therapists were good because, after all, they were well-trained and knowledgeable, came highly recommended, and commanded a high fee. Seemed like a reasonable conclusion, especially if you suffer from unflagging naiveté. Dr. Renway cured me once and for all of my blind faith in her breed. I had gone to her in desperation in October of 2009 for the specific purpose of overseeing my medication, and she had kept up with me through my stay at Alexander during the winter and spring of 2010. When I checked in with her in May after being discharged, she casually offered that maybe she ought to refer me to a psychopharmacologist, a doctor who specializes in medication.

Damn. I said, "Why would you do that—isn't psychopharmacology what you do?" The good doctor: "I don't really specialize in medication; I principally see patients for psychotherapy." We went round and round, but I never got any satisfaction on the issue of my having engaged her purely and simply to oversee my medication.

My own opinion of what ailed me? When I checked into Alexander, I still thought that I had a chemical imbalance that could be treated by drugs. I rationalized, somehow, the fact that in three decades of trying, various doctors hadn't yet hit the right combination or dosage or both. I began to reconsider the idea that drugs could cure me when my treating physician at Alexander took me off of all medication for the first time in years and I actually felt better, not worse. I started to re-examine my life, not my chemistry, for answers.

I realized that, given the degree to which I had been abandoned, betrayed, repressed and subjected to rage as a child, I had developed some coping mechanisms that were harming me more than they were helping. Anyone who knows the story of *The Frog and the Scorpion* will understand when I say that I developed the qualities of both the frog and the scorpion, and my downfall was often attributable to the latter. The fable is one of my favorites:

> One day, a scorpion looked around at the mountain where he lived and decided that he wanted a change. So he set out on a journey, climbing over rocks and under vines until he reached a river. The river was wide and swift, and the scorpion couldn't

see any way across. Suddenly, he saw a frog sitting in the rushes by the bank on the other side of the river and thought to ask him for a ride across. Although the frog was suspicious that the scorpion would sting him, the scorpion convinced him otherwise—after all, he needed the frog alive to get across the river.

So the frog agreed to take the scorpion across. He swam over and allowed the scorpion to climb on his back, then set off to the other side. Halfway across the river, the frog suddenly felt a sharp sting and, out of the corner of his eye, saw the scorpion remove his stinger from his back. A deadening numbness began to creep into the frog's limbs and, knowing that they would both die, he croaked, "Why on earth did you do that?" The scorpion shrugged and replied: "I could not help myself. It is my nature."

Then they both sank into the muddy waters of the swiftly flowing river.[4]

It is easy for anyone who knows me to see me as the frog: that's Suzy, gullible, friendly, eager to please and naturally kind. Left to her own devices, Suzy does just fine in the world; people enjoy her and she appreciates them in return—their humor, their quirks, the surprises they present.

Not everyone has seen the scorpion in me, but for years she was alive and well, intent on self-sabotage in the face of all efforts toward peace, sanity and health. She did not trust others, was suspicious and aloof, and her demeanor did not invite approach. She spent much of her time alone, and Suzy suffered for it.

They did not play well together, my frog and my scorpion. Suzy stayed on guard but was ill-equipped to the task, and my scorpion was always lurking, never out of striking distance. All of this took place, of course, under the mask I wore as my carapace and which in all events is worn by anyone who grows up in the South ("Hi, It's so good to see you, I'm just fine, thank you, and how are you? Got any exciting plans? Well bless your heart, that sounds like so much fu-un").

So, why did I hang on to the scorpion? Or, paraphrasing a line I once read: "What did my madness give me that my sanity had not better provided for?"[5] Such a good line for a semi-addicted bipolar chick with panic disorder, complex post-traumatic stress disorder, treatment resistant depression, maladaptive coping skills and/or mood disregulation. Why didn't I just choose to be sane? The answer was, at that time I couldn't. I didn't yet have the right tools in my toolbox. All I could do was try to keep my sane mind booted up as much as possible, alert for clues that I was getting off track. This required me to patrol my own mind like Big Brother—not an easy way to live, but short of drastic interventions like hospitalizations or shock treatments (which I actually considered), it was the best option available to me as I continued on my quest.

CHAPTER TWENTY-ONE

THE CUCKOO'S NEST

ONCE I GOT acquainted with psychotherapy, it played by far the greatest role in my search for healing. I entered my first real therapy relationship at the age of twenty-nine, and it was a colossal waste of time. Truly, it was like a spoof of therapy, but I didn't know any better at the time and continued to sit across from this well-respected moron and let him stare at me without talking for hours on end for the better part of three years. Every once in a while he would ask me how I felt. Since at the time the only feeling I could identify with any clarity was fear, we didn't make much progress. The only thing I remember of value is that an image came to me almost immediately, an image of an ivy-choked tree and I knew instinctively that it was a metaphor for my psyche—I had to approach my treatment like a tree surgeon unwrapping the tendrils of ivy without disturbing a leaf, like a surgeon unwinding micro-arteries wrapped around a patient's spinal cord. One false move and the result would be paralysis or worse. This was to be an important visual for me to hold on to through the years in the face of my general compulsion to get on with it all and be done with it as quickly as possible.

I got more discerning in picking my therapists as time went on, but the process was achingly slow. Slow didn't work for me, so I branched out. Over time, I tried individual therapy, group therapy, couples counseling, DBT meetings (dialectical behavioral therapy), OA meetings (Overeaters Anonymous), ANAD meetings (Anorexia Nervosa and Related Disorders), nutritionists, weight loss doctors, self-help books and tapes by John Bradshaw and Pia Mellody, yoga, astrology, tarot readings, rolfing, acupuncture, acupressure, tapping (don't ask), and positive affirmations (for a year and a half, every day in my car on the way to work and at night before I went to bed).

Along with therapy, I decided to try to speed things up by adding other cures to my agenda, including every pill, herbal medication, alternative medicine, vitamin and supplement that crossed my path. Other than a couple of six-month periods when I decided to stop taking medication altogether, I was on mood-altering drugs from 1980-2010, thirty long years. Sometimes it was a single drug, often two in combination, and once it was a combination of four. I kept meticulous records (that was the lawyer in me), so I have the complete list from all thirty years. The traditional medications that I took were prozac, wellbutrin, effexor, phen-fen, depakote, celexa, serzone, xanax, paxil, ativan, klonopin, zoloft, cymbalta, topomax, lamictal, geodon, hydrozine, seroquel, phenergan, flexeril, vyvance, trazidone, provigil, lithium, valium, lexapro, resperidone and adderall. In 2002, I read a book on treating mood issues with alternative medicine and over a four month period tried the following supplements, alone and in combination: 5-HTP, L-Tyrosine, Sugar Ban, GTF Chromium, GABA Plus, Magnesium Complex and various multivitamins.

The trial and error associated with prescribing my medication was usually fairly orderly, but during January of 2008, when I was deteriorating fast, my doctors changed my medication seven times in two weeks. I kept a journal: "started Vyvanse, Trazadone and Effexor 1/11/08. Started having symptoms—anxiety, shortness of breath, dry mouth, trembling hands, trouble concentrating and focusing. Stopped Vyvanse 1/13. Still had symptoms. Stopped Trazadone 1/14 per nurse practitioner. Still had symptoms. Restarted Vyvanse 1/16. Stopped Effexor 1/17. Stopped Vyvanse again after a few days—still had extreme anxiety symptoms. Started Zyprexa 1/23."

I would not like to repeat those two weeks. Ever.

I also used to get my thyroid tested from time to time, because thyroid imbalance was a popular explanation for depression and had an easy fix. My thyroid was stubbornly healthy.

I considered various gizmos over the course of time. When I was living in Hong Kong in the 1990s, I almost ordered a special machine that looked like an old-fashioned metal hair dryer without the stand. It was made only in Holland and was going to cost several thousand dollars. It was supposed to provide some new fangled kind of electric shock therapy that seemed quite hopeful to me at the time. I think the fact that it required a trip to Holland to fetch the machine put me off that one, plus I wasn't completely convinced about the electrical part. I did later try a bright light therapy machine; I remember it sitting on my desk in the winter of 2003. It was an encased very bright light that you were supposed to shine directly in your eyes for part of every hour. The idea was for the light to treat seasonal affective disorder, in the event that my depression was brought on by the lack of sunlight. It was irritating and distracted me from my work, and was of no benefit at all that I could tell.

At the same time that I tried the medications and the gizmos, I was voraciously reading every self-help book that I could lay my hands on. They are too numerous to name, but a few come easily to mind: John Bradshaw's *Healing the Shame that Binds You, The Drama of the Gifted Child* by Alice Miller, and *Trapped in the Mirror* by Elan Golumb. I went to a John Bradshaw seminar one time and witnessed one of the saddest things that I have ever seen in my life. One of the exercises at the seminar was to pick a partner and tell them about a terrible thing that had happened to you. I forget what I picked to talk about, but I will never forget my partner's story. When she was a young child (about ten years old), her mother had set up a scenario in which her daughter found her lying on the floor, as if unconscious. When the child tried to wake her mother, the mother pretended to be dead, and would not stop the "game" until her daughter was completely hysterical, absolutely traumatized. Then the mother sat up and said that it had all been a joke. I have heard few stories to equal that, before or since.

Those were the traditional and not-so-traditional therapies and cures that I tried. As I got increasingly desperate, I ventured further and further outside the box, until nothing was out of bounds, whether it was real, imagined, half-baked or germinating as the tiniest seed in someone's unconscious. It was all fair game to me. One of the most peculiar experiences I had during this phase was guided visualizations. They were part of a "course" I took with another woman, complete with a workbook and homework. Together we would lie on mats while our spiritual guide took us through the visualizations, walking through golden hallways and visualizing opening up the tops of our heads so that white energy could pour in through the opening and flow through our bodies and out through our feet, all the way down to the earth's core and anchor us there. Then blue energy was supposed to come in and go out someplace else, and I tried to believe in this and make it work for me, but it was no use: Suzy was in there laughing her ass off, which made it hard to concentrate. The Esteemed Leader of this program would send emails like this:

> Lynn,
> It's been a long time since you've heard from me. I've been in a very inward place since I last communicated with you. It felt like I pierced an energetic membrane and have been soaring through the New Earth space. I bring back good news. The only assignment we have for the next 12 months is to prepare for the Universal Alignment at the end of the year. The way to prepare is to lift up your light quotient.

'Nuff said.

CHAPTER TWENTY-TWO

❧

SUZY'S GREAT ADVENTURE ON THE MOUNTAIN

THE PINNACLE OF MY EXPERIMENTS in non-traditional therapy came in the spring of 2006. I was referred by the therapist whom I was then seeing in Virginia to a mystic named Reverend Dakota Abanoki Asher, a woman who came out of Native American cultural traditions and had achieved renown in alternative circles for her healing abilities. My therapist was heavily into American Indian mythology and healing and a big fan of Reverend Dakota (the reverend part is self-styled), whose bio described her as a Spiritual Dance Elder, Medicine Wheel Healer, Metaphysical Healer, Counselor, Therapist and Spiritual Artist.

At that time, Reverend Dakota also offered a kind of retreat that involved going up to her place on the side of a mountain in northern Tennessee and tuning out the world for a few days in order to go on a "vision quest," a.k.a. revelatory trance/dream. My therapist thought that this might help me clear out the white noise, calm down my system and reconnect me to my center.

I agreed and drove the four hours to Reverend Dakota's mountain in Tennessee. I turned at the driveway whose address I'd been given and drove my minivan up a rutted logging track with potholes the size of craters and equivalent-sized rubble. After what seemed like an hour, when I finally reached the house, Reverend Dakota was not there. I waited for about forty-five minutes before she showed up. She was faintly Indian looking (she was in fact a quarter Indian), with long dark hair and darkish skin. She was shocked that I had driven up the mountain, because she thought that she had left instructions for me to call her on a walkie talkie in her mailbox at the bottom, and she would go down and pick me up. No one had ever made it up there in a regular vehicle. That explained why I was drenched in sweat and my neck was locked in position from hunching over the wheel by the time I arrived at her house. She had gone out and forgotten to leave the note about the walkie talkie, so when I got there I figured I was supposed to go on up.

Now that I was there, we decided that we would worry later about how I would get down, but it was pretty clear that all bets were off if we had a lot of rain over my two and half day stay.

Reverend Dakota's house was a ramshackle place with some huge, filthy Saint Bernard dogs that she raised fenced in next to her porch and a few horses roaming nearby in the tall grass. There was no plumbing and possibly no running water or electricity. There was definitely no toilet, just an outhouse. Devotees would come and work the land and help with repairs, but otherwise the Reverend lived on her own, living off the land for much of the time.

I had come equipped as instructed, with a back pack filled with two rolls of toilet paper, a waterproof tarp, a sleeping bag and a journal. In addition, I had brought two large jugs of water. Reverend Dakota pointed further up the mountain and told me to get started; I needed to be in place by dark. We walked up the hill, with me huffing and puffing and carrying all of my stuff by myself—that was the first part of the drill: no help, take responsibility for yourself. I was overweight and in terrible shape, and it was a really steep hill, so I was already having second thoughts about this particular mission. We went quite a ways, up and up, following a track (not the logging road, but a track), and finally arrived at a bend. To the left she pointed to a space, ten feet round, where I was to set myself up. My instructions were not to leave that circle other than to go to the bathroom for the two and a half days of my stay unless she came to get me. I was given prayer flags in four different colors that I was to tie to sticks facing in the four directions of the compass—it all stood for something, like hope, love and peace. I tried to make the ceremony mean something to me, but it didn't.

I don't know if it was Reverend Dakota who told me that it was a good idea for me to scream at the top of my lungs (sort of like primal scream therapy). I remember doing that on the first night; that is, when it stopped raining and I could come out from being huddled under my tarp. The rain started almost immediately after I settled into my circle and continued steadily for about two hours. All I could do was sit and watch the drops drip off the edge of the tarp that I was holding over my head, the water pooling in the depressions in the ground in my little circle. I wondered how I was going to get my minivan down that fucking mountain in time for carpool the next week. Finally the rain stopped and I set my sleeping bag up as best I could, but it kept sliding down in the mud since my ten-foot circle was at a slight downhill slant.

Before it got all the way dark, I wrote in my journal. The first thing I wrote was about the spiders and bugs that crisscrossed the ground in my circle. They didn't bother me; I'd grown up on what was practically a farm, but I thought about all of my friends who would have died on the spot by then, what with the bugs and the mud and the cold and no food and no toilet but the woods (with the bugs) and the silence.

It was dead quiet. And after the rain stopped, the night sky cleared and it was beautiful. I gave the screaming thing a shot—I had wondered what it was like just to belt it out ever since my friend Coleman told me about primal scream therapy in high school, but I had never had the guts to try it. It's not that easy to do, even with no one around and a whole empty mountain surrounding you. It just seemed so unnatural to scream when I wasn't in danger or afraid of anything. I kept trying because I thought that it would make me feel better, releasing all of that built-up anguish and whatnot, but it didn't; it just hurt my throat. So I had to drink some of my precious reserve of water, which was meant to last me for the whole two and a half days.

I settled down to sleep for my first night ever outdoors under the stars without a tent or any kind of covering. That did feel good. Luckily, this was in the late spring, and even with the rain cooling things off, the temperature was just right. The earth and the wet leaves smelled good. Even the odor of the mud was pleasant. I woke up off and on through the night, and had to go the bathroom in the dark, with just enough light from the moon to see how to get outside of my circle and over to some wet bushes. I stumbled back into the circle and lay back down. I heard a few animals, but I wasn't afraid. I figured Reverend Dakota wouldn't have the reputation she did for hosting these retreats if people were getting eaten by bears.

I woke up in the morning less stiff than I thought I would be, and the weather was fine, if a little misty. About mid-day, Reverend Dakota appeared out of the mist, leaning on a tall walking stick and carrying a bowl of oatmeal for me, a big surprise and very welcome, since I had been told that I would be fasting for my entire stay. I asked her what she thought about the rain and whether I was going to be stuck up there. She said something about the gods and not to worry, that that was part of my job on the mountain, to see that everything could come out okay without me worrying to death about it. She looked at me and said that she could see that I didn't believe in myself, but I should. She was right, I didn't believe in myself and I didn't believe in her encouragement either. She asked me if I had been on a vision quest the night before and I said no, but I had seen shapes in the clouds. I had to say something, I didn't want to appear like a total spiritual dunce, and I really had seen shapes in the clouds—I like doing that.

Reverend Dakota told me about her own vision quest, which of course was a perfect story about journeying far away in a trance and finding something really meaningful which set the course of her entire life and revealed the mysteries of the universe, her totemic animal and everything that she would ever need to know, all in twenty-four hours without ever leaving the place where she was sitting. She told me that not everyone went on a vision quest during their time on the mountain and not to be upset if it didn't happen to me. Naturally, I became obsessed with having this magical thing happen to me and, naturally, it didn't happen.

After I finished my oatmeal, Reverend Dakota took me back down the mountain to sit on some sacred rocks near her house. Don't ask me why they were sacred or what I was supposed to get out of them. I know there were some nettles or sticky brush near one of them, because I scratched the hell out of my arm.

After a couple of hours of doing nothing on the sacred rocks, I went back up to my circle. Later, I heard the voices of men higher up the mountain and that did scare me. I had thought that I was alone on my hillside and was not happy with the idea of company, particularly not of the male variety, that I automatically assumed were on the order of the hill country men portrayed in the film *Deliverance*. After a while their voices faded and I forgot about them. I wrote more in my journal, stared around me, and all of a sudden being on the side of that mountain started to get hard, because I got bored, and then more bored and even more bored. I did not have the habit of being quiet by myself, didn't much like my own company, and this was quite a test for me. I wanted to leave that ten foot circle, I really did, but I hung in there. I took a stone and drew shapes in the dirt, stared out into space, watched my little prayer flags wave in the breeze and waited. Finally, the shadows lengthened and that put me in a better mood, because it meant that I was that much closer to the end of this not terribly fun or, to that point, rewarding, adventure.

Night fell, and I listened to the noises in the woods and the birds. There was very little light in the sky, and I don't remember seeing stars, but I do remember that the sky was very black and it was comforting, because that was how the sky had been at the house where I grew up—not a lot of city lights, always very dark. The ground was hard in places and in others still squishy from the rain, and I kept having to drag my sleeping bag back up after it slid down to the bottom of my little incline. I slept fully clothed except for my boots, which were caked with mud. By this time, I was caked too, if not with mud, with dirt, and a hot shower seemed like a very distant memory. Surprisingly, I wasn't at all unhappy despite the dirt and the uneven ground, because for some reason, the nights were the easiest time. I didn't mind if I woke up in the wee hours; it was so peaceful and such a delight to sleep out in the open, something I hadn't ever expected to do in my life.

The next day, my last day, Reverend Dakota showed up early in the morning and took me down near her house for a visit to the off-duty sweat lodge and the tribal dance clearing. The sweat lodge was cold and the earth was damp, and it was slightly claustrophobic, but it was the first place on the mountain where I felt any touch of mysticism. That was gratifying, because my vision quest clearly wasn't happening and I was running out of time for any grand spiritual experiences. Not that my experience in the sweat lodge was grand, but the place was cave-like and pitch black and I had to crawl into it on my belly under one of the flaps, so I was right next to the earth, and I had a sense of the people who had been there when the coals were hot and the steam was hanging in the air.

The deserted tribal dance clearing, on the other hand, left me cold, so I went back up to my circle to gather my belongings and take them down to my car. I would like to be able to report that it was a bittersweet moment, leaving that circle, but truthfully I couldn't have cared less. Yes, I was proud that I had gutted it out and not fled when I was bored and lonely, but mostly I was glad to be leaving and disappointed that I was coming away with a far less rich experience than I had hoped for.

Before I left, Reverend Dakota again surprised me with food, a delicious meal of corn and vegetables, and I said a polite Southern "thank you for everything," lying through my teeth about how much my time on the mountain had meant to me. We turned and looked at my car, and this time Reverend Dakota had more doubt than I did, because she figured that the rain of a couple of days prior was going to make the trip down even more treacherous than the trip up. I didn't give it a second thought, because nothing in this world was going to keep me from leaving that mountain at that moment.

The drive down was indeed nerve-wracking, but the minivan and I both made it intact, and the feeling of hitting that northern Tennessee country road at the bottom of the mountain was pure bliss. I stopped at a convenience store a couple of miles down the road and the look on the face of the owner when I walked into the store was classic. To say that I was filthy would be a vast understatement—not just my clothes and my boots, but my face, arms, legs, any bit of skin that had been exposed during those two and a half days was covered with mud and dirt. I had the owner take a picture of me. I used to pull it out from time to time, to remind me of Suzy's Great Adventure on the Mountain. Like many of my other forays into non-mainstream therapy, the "retreat to the mountain" didn't take, long term, but if I ever write a book called "Unusual Things that I Have Done," it will be way up there on the list.

CHAPTER TWENTY-THREE

SIGNS FROM ABOVE

T HERE HAVE BEEN TIMES when I have really questioned what the Universe has in mind for me. For example, I found myself in May of 2010 patiently plugging away at pulling myself up out of the mire, and in the space of three days, I got sandbagged twice—well, sandbagged once and reminded of my status as an irretrievable outsider once. First, my art therapy group. It took me months of hunting on the internet to find this group, then weeks of waiting until there was an opening in the group and I could commit to not being out of town for a chunk of time. I thought it would be worth it, though. It recalled the time at Farraday when I found that I could express myself on canvas and I took great pleasure in it and in the comments from the others, their insights based on knowing me in such strangely intimate circumstances.

I had some hesitation about the new art therapy group from the very beginning, but I quashed it, telling myself that I shouldn't be judgmental, take what worked for me and leave the rest. It was hard, though, considering that first out of the box was the lady who kept making images of foxes. They meant something totemic to her, and individually and collectively the group referred to them reverently as "Fox." In the space of a few weeks I saw Fox in clay, oil, and chalk and heard references to him (her?) in various guises such as "Headwaiter Fox." Fine, I had no problem with that, except when we had to give our insights on what we saw in the work.

Here's my insight on Fox. Fox is what they sold me when, tired of not getting any, I went to the local sex shop a couple of months before I joined the group. In response to my question, "What do people use these days for vibrators?" the cute little sales associate took me over to the Wall of Pleasure and directed my attention to the top two bestsellers. The number one bestseller was called "Fox," for the part that has these pointy little ears, split strategically down the middle for functional as well as marketing reasons. Of course I had to have it, to the tune of $100—I might not have been able to come up with bus fare, but I figured this was more in the nature of an investment—long term, by the looks of things.

So when "Fox" popped up in the art therapy group, what could I tell this lady? Top of the line masturbation is all that her Fox in its many incarnations meant to me, but she didn't look like the kind of person who would take this information in the spirit in which it would have been offered. This was a serious bunch, and I had already been chastised twice for not prefacing my insights with "If this were mine, I would ask myself if...." so as to avoid insulting somebody with, God forbid, offensively direct commentary. I was used to the lusty exchange at Farraday, as in, "Wow, that gash of red reminds me of the time you got really hostile when we asked you how you felt about your ex-boyfriend and you told us to fuck off." Those were the good old days.

I bit my tongue and tried to come up with meaningful offerings about Fox, though I don't think they were much help. Still, I hung in there until the straw that broke the camel's back, when we made our Native American drumming journey to honor the move from our current location to a new space. I didn't want to do it; I have done enough of that shit to last me a lifetime with no positive effect that I could see, but I was a good sport and laid my tired middle-aged ass down on the hard floor and dutifully sent my mind forth to seek wisdom and the meaning of everything, doing my best to encounter, as instructed, some significant animals along the way. When we had all returned from our supposed trance states (mine having been a bust, as usual), it turned out that animals, significant or otherwise, had been sorely lacking from the journey at large. This is the comment that the art therapist had to make about that, and I quote: "I wonder with all that's going on in the Gulf [the 2010 oil spill] whether the animals are just showing up to the other animals, and don't have any energy left to show up to people."

Seriously? I mean, seriously? I have worked really hard on my spiritual life, going from nothing to a rudimentary faith of my own making. I have encountered a lot of different variations along the way and am open to lots of possibilities, and I am here to tell you that one of them is not that animals are failing to show up in my dreams because they are running around helping other animals in their dreams and so have nothing left to give me. I just hate shit like that; it makes me want to be sick.

To add insult to injury, the therapist told each of us what vision she had seen for us as we went on our respective journeys. In mine she had seen me walking alone in the desert in blistering heat and two old women came up on either side and walked with me. Boy, that was scintillating. When class ended, I said as much. "Oh," she trilled, "I didn't tell you the rest of it, that you were wearing a red skirt and were really strong and alive and with lots of energy, oh and I am not making that up to make you feel better, I promise." Really?

Installment number two. Two days later, I attended a group for writers. There were eight of us. Whom did I latch onto immediately? The man who had been arrested thirty-three times, had more tattoos than I could begin to count, and showed us the bullet crease on his freshly shaven head. He had brought a sandwich for lunch and pulled out the biggest switchblade I had ever seen to fastidiously cut it down the middle. I watched closely: it was a perfectly clean cut—that sucker must have been really sharp.

What about my background makes me find people like that utterly fascinating? I immediately exchanged email addresses with him and promptly sent him a message, offering to look over his work if he liked. His email response to me was illuminating:

Lynn,
People mentally liberated will encounter friction with the rest of the population. The way you and I see things is oil and water to others. I saw your eyes and smile when u came into the room. Its [sic] almost like a radio station

out there. Most of the time people going about there [sic] day on there [sic] station of choice and sometimes u run into people that are jamming to the exact same frequency you are. You smile happily about the familiar but unknown connection. Like u and I.

He was right. I did find him more interesting than any of the so-called "normal" people in the group, and that's why I sometimes feel so foreign in the world that I inhabit. Take the family dinner a few nights later for my niece's birthday. We were talking about the food, as usual, the quality of the Baskin Robbins ice cream cake, were those real strawberries in the strawberry ice cream and the nuts in the pistachio ice cream didn't taste like pistachios, so were they almonds or what and did that make it pistachio almond ice cream not plain pistachio? Something interesting relating to my friend The Convict popped into my head, and I decided to introduce the topic to see what would happen.

That night had been the opening night of the latest movie in the *Twilight* series, based on the vampire romance novels that had taken the country by storm in 2005. We had already discussed the opening, so the pump was primed. My offering, as soon as there was a lull in the conversation about nuts: "You want to hear something really wild? At the writers group that I went to on Sunday I met a guy who had been arrested thirty-three times and spent a lot of time in jail. He said that the *Twilight* books were hot property in prison among the male population, that who got them first and then the pecking order to follow was a huge deal."

Now, how can that fail to be fascinating, especially if your other choice is almonds? There were four people at the table age twenty and under, and six females. Weren't the odds pretty good that somebody besides me would know what the *Twilight* books were like and get off on the mental image of burly prisoners fighting over books that have passages like, "I'd never seen anything more beautiful—even as I ran, gasping and screaming, I could appreciate that. And the last seven months meant nothing. And his words in the forest meant nothing. And it did not matter if he did not want me. I would never want anything but him, no matter how long I lived"?[6]

Am I the only one who pictures George Kennedy in *Cool Hand Luke* sitting on his bunk, hunched over the book, brow furrowed? All right then, Jean Claude Van Damme in whatever? (I'm sure he has been in a prison flick, how could he have not?)

Guess so. I got some blank stares and a couple of "I don't believe that, I think he was lying to you" remarks, and then, unbelievably, the conversation went back to nuts. I dug my heels in and tried again: "No, really, don't you think it's interesting to think about men in prison reading these books? Can't you just picture it?" Nope, this time I got, "You're really weird!" so I gave up and we went back to nuts. I gave the subject some serious thought and weighed in on the side of the pistachios.

As far as my new acquaintance The Convict was concerned, all I can say is Thank God I made some mainstream friends when I was younger, because more recently I had slipped from the middle of the current to some river two counties over.

Nevertheless, there was a basic truth in what The Convict said to me in his email, and I wonder how apparent that truth is. I wonder how many people have intuited that as shocked as I was by my experiences at Alexander, I also felt good about a lot of what was happening around me. Like being with my friend The Convict, this was exposure to a world of raw action and vitality that I would never have come in contact with but for sliding down the rabbit hole. I have a side that lusts for this kind of intense reality, basks in my connection to it. My problem has always been that, outside of a mental institution, I didn't know how to make that raw world of my desire safe for me to enter. So, out in the world, I stayed away from it, a self-imposed exile of fear, only occasionally tiptoeing close to the edge.

I met a biker in my neighborhood near the end of my time at Alexander. He said he had just moved to Atlanta from Nashville and did the lighting systems for the band Kansas. He was good-looking, shirtless, wearing jean shorts, probably in his late forties, nice body. We talked easily while I walked Henrietta and Horace and he circled his bike back around to catch up with me a few times. We probably could have made some kind of push for it to go somewhere—coffee, a walk, something. I felt the pull; he was part of the "other world" to which I longed to travel, but ultimately I backed off, waving goodbye and walking Henrietta and Horace home. Later, when I left for an appointment, I looked up and down a few streets for his bike, half thinking I would see him and ask if he wanted to meet later for coffee, but he was gone.

CHAPTER TWENTY-FOUR

❧

REAL SIGNS FROM ABOVE

IT TOOK ME MANY YEARS to stitch together the rudimentary belief system that I am still working on today, mostly based on concepts of universality and synchronicity. I have watched things play out in my life that have given me my faith back, albeit in vastly altered form, and I take great pleasure in it.

I rode horses, thoroughbred hunters, for much of my youth, giving it up when I went to college but resuming the sport off and on during my adult years. I bought a retired racehorse when

I was in my late forties, and when I say "retired," I mean old: he was twenty-two years old when I bought him, which is like fifteen or sixteen for a dog. Baron was nevertheless spirited, prone to sudden fits and starts, spooking at shadows and noises, altogether a bracing tonic during the often miserable declining years of my marriage.

One fine day in the early spring, I took Baron for a ride in the outdoor ring. I was not wearing a helmet, because for some reason all the riders at that particular barn thought we were too cool for that, so you rarely saw anyone wearing one. The ground was still hard from the winter and the air was brisk. Baron was jumpy, but I was feeling lazy and after a few turns around the ring, I slowed him to a stop, threw the reins down on his neck, dangled my feet out of the stirrups and leaned back. Whereupon Baron reared up, took off, and flung me hard over the fence headfirst into the ground. The ground should have been like a slab, and so it was all around where I hit, but at the exact point of impact there was a pile of soft dirt that cushioned my fall.

I didn't come away unscathed, sustaining fairly serious nerve damage in my shoulder that required months of therapy, but neither did I have to be airlifted to the hospital, bleeding from my ears, mouth and nose, as did the twenty-one-year-old girl to whom the same thing happened eight weeks later. She was a superb rider, training a young horse, this time in the indoor ring, where all of the dirt is composed of a relatively soft mixture of earth and sawdust. When the horse threw her, she landed on her head in the soft dirt, and still she required emergency brain surgery, went into a coma and, after she woke up, had to have months of intensive therapy to regain her basic motor skills and language.

Was I just lucky?

I started to think not, when, not too long after my fall, another such event occurred. It was at the time of my epic financial reverses, and I couldn't pay the rent. I sold some paintings and jewelry, including a chocolate diamond set of earrings and a ring that I had bought when I lived in Hong Kong. I mentioned the sale to my daughter, Juliana, and she crumbled. Juliana and I had been having a tough time after my divorce, and though we had been working hard to patch things up, our relationship was still precarious. Unbeknownst to me (or forgotten in my post-divorce confusion), the chocolate diamond ring set was precious to Juliana, and my selling it was like a stab in the heart to her.

I scrambled, calling my estate agent friend who had posted the sale on an auction website and pleading with her to get the jewelry back, knowing all the while that I didn't have a prayer in hell of pulling it off. Except I did. It turns out that the buyer lived in Kuala Lumpur and had paid with an

American Express card. At that precise moment, there was a fraudulent scheme in that part of Asia involving the use of American Express cards, and American Express refused to honor the sale, returning ownership of the jewelry to me.

I told Juliana that I had gotten the set back for her, and the look in her eyes told me that we had rebuilt something significant in that moment. It also confirmed my nascent belief that there are very few accidents and fewer coincidences, and that there are mysteries in the world waiting to unfold before me.

The longer I am around, the more I feel drawn to these concepts. It doesn't hurt that in 2001 my therapist told me that I would never get better until I added a spiritual dimension to my life. I took notice of that; it was a pretty strong statement coming from a person who had studiously avoided direct commentary of any kind for the three years I knew her. Her only comments over all that time had been: "What do *you* think about that? How does that make *you* feel?" My unexpressed answers were: "Like I wish you would open your fucking mouth and say something useful once in a while." But she more than made up for it by throwing down the gauntlet on spirituality.

Over time, I have come to believe that there is a universal intelligence that is complicit in what we do, that conspires with us, and I choose to believe that it hopes that we will make choices that are beneficial. The idea is all over the lexicon, always has been, sometimes positive, like the concept of *beshert* (Yiddish for soul mate), sometimes negative, like Murphy's Law and one of my father's favorite Yiddish expressions, butchered in my ignorance, "*mit de pitter arup*" ("the bread always falls with the butter side down"), and sometimes neutral, as in, "I guess it wasn't meant to be." I find all of this tremendously cheering, inasmuch it provides order to what would otherwise be chaos.

From 1950s assimilationist Southern Jewish background to atheist/agonistic (it was hard to lay claim to being a flat-out atheist—it seemed too irrevocable and overly risky) to Universal Intelligence: sounds like a unique journey, but I guarantee you, you could probably find hundreds of thousands like me. I learned some time ago that I was far less special than my ego told me I was. I am the quintessential Baby Boomer, and if I am doing it, thinking it, feeling it, buying it, or saying it, so are the rest of us. Scary, huh?

CHAPTER TWENTY-FIVE

༈

THE MONKEY THERAPIST

WHILE THE EXISTENCE of a benevolent Universal Intelligence is a great concept, I always liked to hedge my bets with help of the human variety, so I was forever going to therapists and buying self-help books. One day I bought a new self-help book about "attachment disorder," that is, what happens when a child doesn't form the normal and critical attachment with his or her primary caregivers. I had read about this from time to time in connection with my own situation, and for some reason was moved on this particular day to circle back to it. The book fell open to page 162, and I read:

> If the trauma, neglect, injury or deprivation is extreme and occurred very early in a person's developmental life, attachment relationships— even powerful ones—cannot always alter a person's damaged neurophysiology. Like the isolated monkeys in Kraemer's (1985) studies who function or look normal as long as they are continually provided for by peer monkey "therapists," once the emotional regulating attachment figure (peer therapist monkey) is removed, the isolated monkeys quickly deteriorate. *The attachment experience that their brains were waiting for, but was never provided, has forever changed the structure of their brain. There are certain changes in the brain that cannot be redressed anymore. Because certain individuals' nervous systems have failed to be exposed to the experience that was supposed to happen, but never did, they will forever require someone else to help keep their nervous system up and running for them.* They will always require an abundant

amount of external affect regulation. With certain individuals, a long-term therapeutic holding environment, like the one that AA provides the alcoholic, will always be necessary.[7]

Ergo, I was doomed. Unless, that is, I got my very own therapist monkey, one to be with me all of the time, to psychoanalyze me on command, be my companion and friend, to watch T.V. with me, but only the shows I wanted to watch, who would not object to marathon sessions of *Dog, The Bounty Hunter*, to interact, to distract, to help and to BE THERE, all of the time.

Did I mention that I needed this magical being to be there all of the time?

The ideas of "help" and responsibility were problematic for me for most of my life. I thought I was entitled to be helped and that other people, particularly family, were responsible for my well-being. This way of thinking almost cost me my relationships with my two older children, David and Juliana, who bore the brunt of my neediness in the months before I went to Farraday. The worse I felt, the more I leaned on them, and when they quite rightly refused to act as my monkey therapists, I confronted them weekly if not daily with great drama, demanding that they engage with me in what were to them utterly maddening discussions about their feelings for me. I could see that every time I did this it was driving them further away instead of closer to me, but I couldn't understand why and I couldn't stop myself. I railed against the gap that was widening between me and my children, a gap that seemed to me unbridgeable. Friends and counselors explained to me over and over that I was the parent and they were the children, and that it was wrong for me to reverse the roles and ask them to take care of me. I didn't get it; the concept was as foreign to me as if you had suddenly asked me to start speaking Swahili. I was alone and in trouble, and my children were my closest family. If I was down and out, they were supposed to take care of me, no questions asked, no matter that they were only fifteen and seventeen years old. Right?

No, not right at all. It took me years to come to terms with this notion, and years of mutual effort with my children to rebuild our relationships and regain each others' trust, but I later came to understand that everyone else, my children included, had been right and I had been wrong. As I was to figure out later, I was in Suzy Marmalade mode at her most flawed, and that one of the worst things a parent can do to a child is to demand that the child parent him or her instead of the reverse. It is completely out of the natural order of things and if my children had succumbed to my demands, it could have screwed them up royally. Lucky for me, they were wiser than I in this particular domain, had a stable father and good instincts for self-preservation, so with some bumps and bruises, they made it out intact, and as a family we later healed the wounds that I had inflicted.

My children weren't the only people I expected to save me at that time. One of the more poignant but also slightly silly moments to me at Farraday was when I confronted my therapist, Dr. Finster, angry that he was doing a lousy job and that he wasn't helping me, which was his inescapable duty. Wrong again on all counts: this man was brilliant, he knew exactly what he was doing and he was helping me, just not the way I wanted him to. I wanted him to fix my problems immediately and by himself. He said no, I needed to help myself, which I rejected literally by taking myself off in a huff to art class and making a large box, which I took to my next session with him. I got inside the box and refused to come out until Dr. Finster extended his hand to help me up. I drew pictures, too, that I brought him as supposed proof that he was wrong, infantile drawings of dogs in cages and people helping them to get out. Like I said, Suzy had hunkered down and wasn't going anywhere at that time without the help she thought she deserved. Luckily, in his own way, Dr. Finster obliged.

CHAPTER TWENTY-SIX

SUZY STEPS OUT OF THE BOX

WHEN I WASN'T DEVOTING my time at Farraday to hiding in boxes, I learned a thing or two from Dr. Finster that were important to my recovery. I am sure that these things had been said to me at various times in various ways by other therapists, but one thing I have learned about the therapeutic process is that nothing sticks until you are ready to hear it. I guess I was finally ready. The first revelation came when he pointed out that, because of the dynamics in the household in which I grew up, I was out of step with time—early in some respects and late in others, but rarely on time. My teaching was neglected as a small child, to the point that at the age of four I still didn't know my colors or that a proper stool required three legs—that's why I failed the entrance exam to kindergarten at the school my parents wanted me to attend. Yet I was an "old soul" from the time that I can remember and had an odd capability to laser in on the truth of a situation even as a child.

Dr. Finster's explanation made sense to me and paved the way for my first feelings of compassion toward myself. I was screwed up? I had issues? Well of course I did! What would you expect of someone who never held a baby until she was thirty and yet had two of her own by thirty-six? How could I have been on track, reaching life's milestones right on time? His explanation also shed new light on why I had lived my life the way I had. As a rider and horse lover, I was always reading books about horses from the time I was able to read, and early on I read that the way to jump a horse over a fence was to throw your heart over the fence first and follow after. That's what I did in all areas of my life for so many years, because I knew intuitively that if I waited for the right time, the moment when I felt in sync, I was going to run out of time before I ever tried anything. I did it with law school, marriage, having children, raising children, jobs and about anything else you want to name that has anything to do with living life. I threw my heart over the fence and hoped for the best. More often than not it all turned out fine.

The second eye opener from Dr. Finster was his appraisal that I had been the "identified patient" in my family for my entire life. The concept of the identified patient means that one person in the family unit gets to carry all the underground baggage for the whole family for all time unless and until that person does enough work to walk away from it and leave everyone else to sort themselves out. It allows everybody else to pretend that they don't have issues, because there is always someone else to point the finger at.

Understanding that I had filled that role was a big step toward objectivity and it brought with it a healthy sense that it wasn't necessarily I who had derailed. I had always been an intrinsically calm and lucid, if somewhat sensitive, person, but my underpinnings had been weakened and my resiliency undermined growing up in a less than nurturing environment. If I had spent decades on the couch and served my time "inside," that said less about me than it did about the environment that had produced me. I once found the most wonderful quote in support of this belief: "That a person has undergone psychotherapy must not be perceived as an indication of emotional impairment. It may actually indicate reasonableness, courage and emotional maturity. I have never found my patients to be a sicker population than my circle of friends."[8]

Damn straight.

Another thing that provided a good deal of release for me was when, encouraged by Dr. Finster, I called Amelia to get a fresh account of the circumstances surrounding her abrupt disappearance from my life, along with George and Pamela. George had died in the 1980s, but I had stayed in touch with Amelia and Pamela off and on over the years and had visited Amelia's home several times. On those visits I would usually corner Amelia and ask her what had happened, why they had left the way they did, but her answers had always been vague and incomplete. Anyway, I never could remember exactly what she had said—it was always too hard to hear her words and retain them at the same time. This time I wrote down her answer, because I wanted to know once and for all and never have to ask again.

After Amelia answered my call and we said a quick hello, I demanded, "So, when I was thirteen and you all left, what happened? Why did you leave?"

> Amelia: George went into a business and he stopped coming to the house. Our leaving was his fault. Your mother had to hire somebody else. I worked a while after George stopped, but after a while your mother needed help she could count on.
> Me: Why did you leave and not say goodbye?

Amelia: I was sick—I stayed in the hospital with the mumps. I got so swollen I couldn't see. A rash came over my eyes and I couldn't stand the light and I had such a dry mouth, I couldn't eat anything but liquid. I stayed there for some time and one day I was walking down the hall and I couldn't stand up, I blacked out.

Me: Why did you leave and not say goodbye?

Amelia: I didn't get to see you any after I got sick. We moved out of your house into the little house down the way. So much was going on and I had the two kids and George was drinking.

Me: Did it occur to you the impact it would have on me?

Amelia: Yes, but your mother had other people up there at the house and I just didn't want to go up there. Your mother had decided that she needed to be around you more and I didn't want to interfere. It was hard for me and I just cried over leaving you—you all were my life and I just loved every one of you and I felt I would be there 'til I died. I went through a lot. I loved every minute I stayed there and your mother and father were so nice to us. But you weren't there and after I left I didn't go back up to the house to see anyone. It just broke my heart.

Me: Was it that you couldn't think of what to say to me?

Amelia: No, it wasn't that I couldn't think of what to say to you, it was because I didn't see you. I didn't even see you anymore. I don't remember seeing you anymore after we moved down to the other house on the property. I don't remember you ever coming down there. That didn't stop me from loving you and caring about you, you and your brother both—you all were my life. I used to dress you up and bring you down to the dinner table and they would look at you and you would sit there for a few minutes and then I would take you back up. That's the only time your father saw you. I would dress you up and curl your hair. I would read you stories every night before you went to bed. Or have you recite the 23rd Psalm—I taught you how to do that and you could recite the whole thing when you were three years old.

At this point we wrapped up our conversation, Amelia seemingly unaware that I was dismayed, even shell shocked, by her words. To hear Amelia keep saying "I didn't see you" was brutal. Amelia was one of the few people in the world to whom I thought I was visible down to my core. The only thing that held me together during the youngest part of my life was the reflection that I saw in her eyes, the reflected love and acceptance, the way she saw me that the rest of my family didn't—beautiful and whole, no parts missing, nothing to criticize. For her to tell me that she didn't say goodbye to me because she "didn't see me anymore" hurt badly. I couldn't figure out how she could say that she didn't see me—I had been there, like always, in the house where I grew up; it's not as if at age thirteen I had moved out and joined the traveling circus.

As if that were not bad enough, the conversation provided an unpleasant reminder of just how distant my own parents had been, how truly invisible I was to them as a child. Juggling my reaction to Amelia's stories of how I was brought downstairs like a trained bear, dressed up for show, and then retired to my room when I ceased to be amusing, with my reaction to the news that she hadn't "seen" me, left me reeling, almost like a physical assault.

But when I thought more about our conversation, a few things became apparent, and I also figured out some subtext that worked for me, true or not. I could understand the idea that if my mother had decided to take over the raising of me, Amelia would not feel comfortable interfering. That made complete sense to me. And at thirteen years old, I did have my own life. I went horseback riding way out in the country at least four days a week, was busy with my friends and school, and I am sure that I wasn't "there" the way I had been when I was younger. The subtext that I read was that, while that's a natural separation for a mother and a daughter, Amelia may have been hurt that I didn't need her as I had in the past. Every mother goes through that pain, but the timing of Amelia's departure was particularly unlucky for both of us, because it took what should be a natural process of separation over time and severed it overnight with a surgeon's scalpel.

What hurt the most was that Amelia had so many other things going on in her life at the time that it is entirely possible that she really didn't think about me. It reminded me of my description of myself at Juliana's graduation. When you are in that spot, if you have any instinct for survival at all, you get very selfish, because otherwise you know that you may not make it out alive, or at least that's how it feels. I, of all people, knew the truth of that.

Whatever my reaction, I felt that for the first time I had probably gotten a much closer approximation of the truth surrounding Amelia, George and Pamela's departure. This time there was context for what had happened, and all the players were complex and their lives were complicated, and that was something that I could believe in and start to include in the fabric of my memory. And the healing could begin.

PART FOUR

THE ART OF LIVING

CHAPTER TWENTY-SEVEN

MY KIND OF GUY

WHILE I MADE PROGRESS on some fronts with Dr. Finster, one area that lagged behind was my relationships with men. He made great efforts to focus me on problems he perceived in that area, but I didn't have the energy for it and only dimly recognized why he thought it was such a big deal anyway. So what if I was doomed to repeat past failures, attracted as I was to anti-heroes, with baggage to match? I was focused on staying alive, not finding a date. Time would prove that Dr. Finster was right, that this was a very big piece of the puzzle for which I needed to find a place, but I wouldn't see the shape of the piece or where it fit in the puzzle for another two years.

My issues with the opposite sex showed up early in my life, in third grade to be exact, the year that I married my "boyfriend," Coleman, with a crinoline petticoat as a veil and a bubble gum machine toy as a ring. Ah, Coleman. He was the love of my life all through grade school, on into high school and beyond. He was a gorgeous boy and turned into the most polite, refined, well-spoken smack freak (heroin addict) you would ever want to meet, still handsome until he lost all the weight, got acne from the drugs and turned bi-sexual (in other words, became a scag fag—does anybody else remember '60s drug addiction slang?). My mother was taken with him as well. What mother wouldn't be? He had better manners than Wally in *Leave it to Beaver.*

As the smartest kid in the grade, I was class president by acclamation from third through fifth grade. In sixth grade I had to run formally, and my opponent was Coleman, now the most popular boy in the class. I was already well into Suzy mode, so when he came up to me in the cafeteria and asked why I hadn't put up any posters like the ones with which he and his friends had plastered the walls, I had no idea what he was talking about. Needless to say I lost the election, but I walked away happy that we'd had a conversation.

I transferred schools in seventh grade and saw Coleman only rarely until the summer after high school. That summer we became friends again and I got a close-up view of the life of a teenage drug addict. I helped him shoot up one time, tied the rubber tourniquet tight on his arm as he inserted the needle. I was under his sway, he was an enormously charismatic person by anyone's account, and I'm lucky he only asked me politely if I wanted a hit myself. If he had exerted any pressure at all I am sure I would have shot up, which, given my addictive proclivities, would not have been a good thing at all.

That same summer Coleman stole a valuable ring from me, an opal and diamond ring that my grandparents had given to me for my sixteenth birthday. I knew he had taken it because we had been looking at my jewelry that afternoon. I have always been like a crow when it comes to anything shiny, so I loved to play with my jewelry and didn't care who I did it with, still don't. I would invite the mailman in to play with my jewelry if I thought he would come. I noticed that the ring was missing that night and, in a move that was uncharacteristically confrontational for me, I called Coleman up and accused him of stealing it. He denied it at first, but I was on the warpath and didn't let up. He later called back and said that he had found the ring; he must have taken it by accident and would return it the next day. He did, and I felt a rare sense of power over him in particular and the world in general.

That summer was also notable for Coleman's attempt to teach me how to kiss. I remember it wistfully. I wish that he had done a better job and that I hadn't been so scared. I wish I could have connected better with this boy who was reading *Primal Scream* and *The I Ching* while I, under my mother's tutelage, was buried in Victorian romances. I wish my devotion could have been enough to save him from the drugs, but I don't know if anyone could have, and skating on my own thin ice, I surely didn't have a chance.

I saw Coleman only one time after that summer, ran into him at a mall when we were in our twenties. He looked awful, and it was hard to find any trace of the gorgeous boy I had known. I thought about Coleman once in a while over the years that followed and on a whim called his sister in 2003. She told me that he had died in the late 1990s, and while that should not have shocked me, it did. I saw myself in him, only he recognized his demons so much earlier than I did. I wish he had won the battle. I wish I could talk to him about it now that I myself had become so deeply engaged.

Besides Coleman, "my kind of guy" included a range of what I can only describe as "fill in the blank-sexual": heterosexual, homosexual, bisexual, metrosexual, and any other kind of sexual, as long as they were sophisticated. I traveled all over Europe during my junior year in college with a gay friend named Douglas who was brilliant. He spoke all of the Romance languages except Romanian, plus some German, at age twenty. He also had wonderful jewelry, along with a tremendous wit and sense of humor. I used to go with him to the clinic in Paris where he had electrolysis done on his facial hair. In the 1970s this was not a fun affair—the needle was about the size of a large safety pin and I know it hurt like hell—but Douglas was determined.

Of all of the countries to which we traveled, the Iron Curtain countries really spooked Douglas. He was obsessed with the notion that the soldiers and police we saw were itching to throw him in prison, visiting American or not, and it became a real pain in the ass trying to cross a street with him. No matter where we were when the little pedestrian signs changed from green to red, he leapt back up on the curb like a gazelle stung by a bee, and I had to wait through the traffic cycle all over again. As a result of his paranoia, my memories of Bucharest are mainly of curbs and traffic lights, so I suppose I'll have to go back if I want to see anything more of the city.

After college, Douglas and I lost touch, and I didn't make any new gay friends until I hired a decorator named Riley to work on the condo I moved into after law school. He was hugely gifted with design, funny as hell and vastly entertaining. One time when I came home from taking some courses at University of Miami Law School, he offered to pick me up at the airport. I said "Great," and when I walked out of baggage claim, there was Riley, all 6 foot 2 inches of him, in a long brown wig, a sea green formal gown and size 13 heels, leaning against the fins of his 1959 Cadillac. I had overlooked the fact that it was Halloween, but I don't think I would have expected the vision of Riley in full drag at the airport even if I had remembered.

When it came to picking the man who would be the central character in my adult life, I headed straight for the consummate metrosexual—Leo had it all, long before the term was invented. He dressed impeccably, had gorgeous manners and was the ultimate sophisticate—widely traveled, fluent in French and a connoisseur of food, wine, and art. Leo was darkly handsome to boot, often mistaken for Italian or Greek, although his forbears were one hundred percent Lithuanian. (Personally, I always suspected that some Cossack was thrown into the gene pool after a midnight ride down from the steppes one cold winter night.) Whatever parts of our marriage were less than perfect, it was not the parts that related to a mutual love of *la dolce vita*; there, we were completely in sync, and it's something that I have not yet succeeded in replacing. That I often waste my time looking in all the wrong places might be the problem.

CHAPTER TWENTY-EIGHT

❧

INTERNET DATING IN THE FIFTIES

I NTERNET DATING IN MY FIFTIES, that is. I was fifty-three years old, and it was after I got divorced and had been living on my own for a while. I joined a group of newcomers to town on meetup.com, figuring that being divorced was pretty much like being new to town and maybe I'd meet some interesting people at the events. I went on a few outings, notable among them the time when I went to an event at a big screen movie theater, had a panic attack and ended up with my ex-husband

and daughter coming to pick me up off the floor and cart me back to my house. I've had a few of those attacks in my life and I find their timing interesting. The first occurred when I was having a massage in Portugal. The second one was when I was on a skiing vacation in Colorado. The third, not one but a series, woke me up out of a sound sleep every night for weeks while I was living in Hong Kong. Is there something about relaxation that is foreign to my system?

There came a day when I posted a message on the meetup.com group message board asking if anybody liked Crosby, Stills, Nash and Young and wanted to go to a concert with me. I got an answer from some guy who said he didn't like CSNY but he did like electric guitar and soon we were happily chatting away. He was divorced, I was divorced, we liked the same kind of music, both enjoyed traveling, food, books: ain't life grand? A week or two later we graduated to exchanging our private email addresses and before I knew it, I had embarked on my first internet dating venture. Unbeknownst to me, I was the littlest Billy Goat Gruff to my soon-to-be boyfriend's Troll under the bridge. If you aren't familiar with the old Norwegian fable, just plug in the part in *Jurassic Park* where the goat is staked out as dinner for the T Rex.

At first he couldn't meet me for a month or so, because he was going away on a cruise. It was too expensive to call from the ship, so we couldn't have contact at all. My therapist, of all people, pointed out that this was odd, since to her knowledge it was cheap to call from on board ship, but I said that she must be wrong. After all, why would Donald lie?

When he came back, we were supposed to meet, but he got tied up repairing the toilet of the elderly couple next door, nice guy that he was, so he couldn't make it. More emails, more phone calls, lots of pseudo-romance, which I ate up with the shovel it was served on. A few nights later, we finally met for coffee. By this time, I was in fantasy land, so the fact that he turned out to be a chain-smoking stand-in for an apprentice coal miner, pot belly and slouch included, was not even relevant. (But he was tall, let's not overlook that he was tall.) I do remember blinking a couple of times, hard, then shrugging it off, and grabbing the brass ring with hands outstretched.

Did I say ring? Oh yeah, it was about this time that Donald emailed me a picture from the cruise, and I responded, "What's that ring on your left hand, are you married?" "Oh no, oh my gosh, let me turn that around and take a picture of it that way and send it to you, that's my high school ring." Well of course it was, he had already said that he was divorced, so why would it be a wedding ring?

We had a few more dates, and I started wondering why I was never invited over to Donald's

house. I asked him about this, and he said that he
was moving, and I would come over to the new
place. In the meantime, we planned a romantic
getaway to a nice hotel, and I was mollified. Until
he called me that afternoon, in tears, yes, tears,
that he had gone out on a boat with a friend earlier
in the day and been stung by a bee, and gone to
his neighbor who had given him medication for
the sting, but he was allergic to the medication
and he was falling asleep, but before he fell asleep
he made the friend dial my number, because he
was worried, yes so worried, and so upset that
he couldn't be with me, and that was why he was
crying.

I hardly knew what to think, and if I sound
naïve (okay, dumb), it's because a) I was still in the
role of the littlest Billy Goat Gruff in the fairy tale),
b) Suzy believes that people tell the truth, and (c)
he was glib. Glib? Is there a word for more than
glib, preposterously glib, world class, Olympian
glib? In this, Donald was in a class of his own: he
was Bernie Madoff in overalls.

I went to Barnes and Noble the next day for
coffee and a soothing browse through the new crop
of serial killer novels. I stopped by the information
desk to ask a question and struck up a conversation
with the woman in front of me. We adjourned to
the in-store Starbucks for coffee, and I told her the
Donald story. She looked at me for a moment and
said, "I don't know you, so I hope you don't take

this the wrong way, but I think that your boyfriend is married."

Ding Ding Ding Ding Ding. The lady had a point: there were too many holes in Donald's story to be plausible, and I determined to follow up with a little detective work. I called the hotel that was to have hosted our aborted tryst. No reservation in his name, nor my name, nor my cat's name, not the day of, the day before, the day after, the week before or the week after. County records where he lived: no record of a divorce under his name, first or last. County records where he was moving: same result.

On the urging of a friend, I drove out to the address that Donald had given me of his old house, the house where he had lived before he moved. I turned into a cul-de-sac and, while there was no sign of his car at the address I had, why there it was, big as life, right next door. I got out of my car and I went to the house at the end of the cul-de-sac and rang the bell. A woman answered and I said: 'You see that house over there, do you know Donald who lives there?" "Yes." "Is he married?" "Yes, his wife's name is Karen."

I had to sit down for a while to take that in, but presently I summoned up my persona as Biggest Billy Goat Gruff, which lurks in my depths for just such occasions, and walked up to Donald's house and rang the bell. He answered the door, took one look at me and stepped out fast, pulling the door shut behind him. "This is bad timing," he said, "I'm having a big argument with my ex-wife." Like I said, he was nothing if not quick on his feet with a lie. "That's not your ex-wife, that's your wife, I asked Sally down at the end of the street." We haggled over it for a while, until he finally admitted that he was married, which for some reason was important to me. So I walked away and that was that.

I always felt bad that I couldn't make Donald wear a sign or something to warn all of the other unsuspecting littlest goats out there, but that's not how it works. I guess the littlest goats get what they deserve, unless they go the *Eat, Pray, Love* route, in which case they attract cute guys who are a decade or so younger who stare at them soulfully until they decide to dump them in favor of food, ashrams and, finally, suitably aged men who stare at them soulfully; but then if that happens, they're not the littlest goats, now are they?

CHAPTER TWENTY-NINE

A CAUTIONARY TALE

A FTER DONALD, I was put off of guys for a while, but after a time, I decided to give a dating service called "It's Just Lunch" a shot. The idea was that the service matched you up on a date for lunch or drinks, and if there was no chemistry, at least you hadn't invested, God forbid, a whole evening in it, not to mention the cost of a dinner. The chivalry that I was raised with is mostly dead, and I can't really say whether I think that is a good or a bad thing. I have read *Super Sad True Love Story* by Gary Shteyngart and if that's anything to go by, whatever the new chivalry will be, if at all, it will likely be something I can barely imagine, like acquiescing to someone's choice of which app to use on their date's iPhone to pick a restaurant.

The first two outings were duds. On my third try, the plan was to meet my date at a bar for drinks after work. It was a nice bar, and I was a little excited. I approached the hostess and said that I was there to meet a date from "It's Just Lunch" and could she please point him out. She pointed out a solitary gentleman seated at the bar, in a short-sleeved white shirt, skinny tie and glasses, looking for all the world like an IBM computer nerd from the 1960s. I almost bolted, but good manners overtook me and I went up and introduced myself to Ben. I sat down, tossed down a couple of drinks and soon I was half listening to him through an alcoholic haze, sort of bored but not as much as I thought I'd be. Offhandedly, well into the conversation, I asked Ben what he did for a living. "I'm a rocket scientist."

Well now. Even in my stupor, that caught my attention, and I asked him a few questions to see if he was joking. He wasn't; he had worked for NASA for years in the field of astrophysics or something equally incomprehensible to me. I never expected to meet, much less date, a rocket scientist, and I was mightily impressed with him and with me. I'm a sucker for a really smart guy, meaning some combination of intellect, common sense and emotional intelligence; in fact, if I were to make a short list of my "relationship requirements," that would be at the top and it might in fact be the only thing on the list. I can compromise on short, tall, overweight, underweight, long hair, short hair, jobless (let's call it "in between jobs"), some alcohol, some drugs, and, as demonstrated, any number of mental health irregularities ranging from minor peccadilloes to full-blown psychosis, but I have to draw the line somewhere, and I draw it at brains. (Although if Tommy Lee Jones or Johnny Depp turned out to be dumb, I might make an exception.)

Things lasted a while with my NASA friend but ultimately didn't work out, and I soon became more preoccupied with keeping body and soul together than the opposite sex. Some time after I came out of the years of gloom, though, I regained my interest in dating and joined eHarmony, late 2010 or thereabouts. It didn't take long before I hit what I thought was pay dirt, receiving a message from a man whose profile indicated that he was a doctor and a writer, and that his favorite book was James Joyce's *Ulysses*. If I was looking for a really smart guy, this had to be the cream of the crop, I thought, and I was hopeful that something good would materialize.

We started communicating through the canned eHarmony questions: "What would you rather do on a Saturday night? What bothers you most in a partner? How many books did you read last year?

(between zero and three books is an option on the selection list, which I find hard to believe.)

Once we made it over the initial hurdles and on to the open-ended questions, he asked me about my writing, what kinds of things I wrote about. I looked through my manuscript and had a hard time finding a chapter that was suitable to send to a stranger. "Suzy Marmalade Goes Inpatient (Again)?" No. "Suicide by Blender?" No. "Do Not Date Another Patient?" Hardly. I finally settled on the excerpt about the art therapy group, the part about the iconic Mr. Fox, with a mere hint of my visit to the sex shop. I figured we were adults, after all, and this *was* a dating website, so you were supposed to allude to romance and the like, right?

What I got back from my would-be suitor as an illustration of his own writing took me aback. He sent me three chapters, the contents of which reminded me painfully of passages from the Victorian romances of my youth. But this man's writing was worse, roughly comparable to *The Scarlet Pimpernel* on crack. One chapter also included a description of a clinical procedure performed on a woman that totally disgusted me.

I fired off an email defending my honor as a lady: "I was really uncomfortable that you sent me material with so much sex in it; I don't even know you. I know I opened the door with my little 'excerpt.' It may have given you the wrong impression, and if it did, I'm sorry." I said that I was interested in meeting the man whose favorite book was *Ulysses*, not the man who had written such tripe (I did not use the word "tripe," but I was pretty strong). He gave an explanation about the material he had sent me, something about it being clinical and necessary to the plot, and he was a doctor and so on, and accepted my criticism with good grace. With the urging of a few misguided friends, I swallowed my misgivings and agreed to meet for drinks.

What followed was the blind date to end all blind dates, the cautionary tale of all cautionary tales. This is the one that every mother should recount to her daughters when invoking the dangers of dating in the twenty-first century, particularly internet dating.

From the minute I met Warren, I noticed a disconnect. A blind date is generally uncomfortable, true, but in this case there seemed to be a level of normal human connection that was missing. His team had just won the Super Bowl—no reaction. We had children about the same ages—no reaction. He lived next door to a man who had gone to law school with me, still a good friend—no reaction. I asked him about his medical practice, which I had found on Google and looked interesting. He responded without inflection that he hadn't practiced for the last ten years, since he had been raising his children in a few different cities as a single parent since his wife died twelve years ago.

Sometimes I have a bad memory and sometimes I have a sterling memory. This time it was the latter, so I said, "What do you mean, your wife died, I thought you were divorced? I read in your profile that the biggest influence in your life was your ex-wife." His response: "Well, we weren't divorced when she died, does that mean that we weren't divorced?" I looked at him: a man whose favorite book was *Ulysses* thought that it was possible to get divorced after your spouse died? I let it go and we talked a little longer—about kids and writing and his wife's death. She had suffered a cardiac event while the family was on vacation in Brazil, unexpected and very sad.

After a while, it was clear that neither of us had any interest in pursuing things, so we shook hands at the end of the evening and parted company. Still, something had piqued my curiosity, and the next day I called our mutual acquaintance from my law school days. We chatted for a minute and then I asked my friend what he knew about Warren. More than I had bargained for, as it turned out. Before moving to Atlanta, Warren had been convicted for Medicaid fraud and had gone to prison. Okay, that explained why he hadn't practiced medicine for ten years. We talked a bit more and it turned out that my friend had known Warren's wife as well and confirmed that she had died in Brazil of an allergic drug reaction.

I counted myself well out of it all and went off to lunch with my friend, Deborah. I gave her the outlines of the story; we laughed, and then moved on to other things. At the end of the lunch, something made Deborah come back to it and ask: "By the way, you know the man you went out with last night, how exactly did his wife die?" To which I replied, "I'm not sure. They were in Brazil and I think it was some kind of an allergic reaction that caused a heart attack." She stopped in her tracks, speechless for once (Deborah was not often at a loss for words), and finally blurted out, "Oh My God!" and grabbed my arm. "She didn't die. He killed her!"

She explained: "I heard about this guy, years ago. A lot of people thought that he had killed his wife. He had her cremated in Brazil before an autopsy could be performed." A friend had told her that Warren was even under investigation by the government for insurance fraud when he collected the proceeds of his deceased wife's life insurance, but there was no proof, since he had handily disposed of the body. Two or three months later, his neighbors reported that Warren was building a tennis court in the back yard of his house, presumably with those same insurance proceeds.

All righty then. I had attracted an ex-con who might have been a suspected killer—not bad for my first time back in the fray. The good news was that from that baseline there was nowhere to go but up, and I made the further decision to get more aggressive and make the first contact if someone was appealing, a bold departure from my southern belle upbringing. As time went on, I became quite proud of myself, both that I was taking the initiative and that I was able to take the expected percentage of non-responses and outright rejections in stride.

Things went fine until I became fixated on a certain political figure in the midst of my quest, to the point that a prospective suitor's opinion of that figure became my screening question on the website. Up until then, my politics had been almost non-existent; if anything, I had been a left-leaning centrist who wanted to have it all ways—yes, we should have a war machine, we're supposed to be the protector of the less fortunate around the globe. Yes, we need all social services and especially help for the mentally ill. (I had to have my special interest, doesn't everybody?) Yes, we should have a balanced budget. Yes, we should promote jobs at home. Yes, we should be able to buy things as cheaply as possible.

Since even I knew that you couldn't have all of those things at the same time, I usually stayed away from politics, realizing that I knew too little to have an informed opinion. So it was quite out of character for me to take a stand to the point that I wouldn't date someone who would admit to respect for this politician, but there it was—I was adamant. To my shock and chagrin, I began losing date prospects right and left. Some pollster would find this very interesting, but to me it was very disappointing, although on the positive side, the experience led to thoughts of a possible new career as an advocate against this particular politician.

An example of an exchange:

Me: I liked your profile, some of your comments were really funny. I like to email instead of sending the canned questions, seems more personal. Take a look at my profile and if it looks interesting, send me a message. And now for my screening question. Are you a Ms. X fan? If so, I still like your profile, but I don't think this is going to work out. :-)

Cheerful, right? Positive, yes? Not overly confrontational, little smiley face at the end to show that I'm cool with it all, no harm no foul, just a parting of ways that never came together to begin with. Wrong. Here's the response I received: "I voted for Ms. X in the last election. Bye now."

Okay, a little frosty, no need to be flip, but whatever. But no, this wasn't the end of it; apparently I had really hit a nerve. Eleven minutes later, having presumably stewed over my perceived attack on the object of this man's esteem, he wrote more:

Did you vote for King Pie in the Sky and his merry band of thieves and thugs? I have many, many years of experience teaching business and economics and consulting with businesses, large and small, so I am well informed [let me insert—"and a pompous ass"]. King Pie in the Sky isn't...but he has charisma and slogans!

It took me a while (Suzy was at the helm at the time) to figure out whom he was even talking about. I really had no idea. Finally it dawned on me that he was venting about our current president, Barack Obama, a fairly common pastime of the day. That was his prerogative, but I thought it an overreaction to my simple, non-emotionally laden question. The real surprise came when I found that he wasn't the only one to shoot me down; they all did, every single man I picked, and after about seven, I started wondering whether I needed to move to a different region of the country. Of course, my mother pointed out after reading the manuscript for this book that after I divorced Leo, she had developed grave concerns about my man-picking ability, so I guess I was nothing if not consistent.

P.S. Twist my arm, I have to admit that the object of my fixation was Sarah Palin. Tar me, feather me, hang me from the rafters, I cannot abide that woman and do not for the life of me understand how anyone can. I do, however, appreciate the opportunity that she gave Tina Fey to provide me and countless others with a moment of unparalleled humor as she lampooned Ms. Palin on *Saturday Night Live.* If Ms. Palin was to deprive me of a social life, at least she gave me something worthwhile in return. I could almost like her for it, but then again, not.

CHAPTER THIRTY

GIVE THAT WOMAN A JOB

D ATING ASIDE, I had more serious concerns at that time in my life. Ranked highly among them was that I found myself "temporarily embarrassed." That's an old-fashioned phrase that perfectly describes how I felt about my situation in the summer of 2010: back in Atlanta, impoverished, one step away from going on the dole with my mother, rejected by prospective employers at every turn and living in an apartment with uneven floorboards and no thermostat. I love this particular usage of the word "embarrassed."

It was often used in the Victorian novels I read as a teenager, the very same novels that introduced me to "the vapors" (only spelled "vapours" in the English way). The typical context was when a young dandy found himself "temporarily embarrassed" at the gaming tables, that is, out of money or credit, but sure to re-establish himself in short order.

In my current condition, it was the last part that I wasn't too sure about, the "re-establishing in short order," and it turned out that my hunch was right. For an entire year, I applied for dozens of jobs, with no responses except the one that turned out to be an Australian drug dealer and the one where the person who responded was trying to commit identity theft.

The former was posted on Craigslist by a man who lived "mostly in Australia," whatever that meant, and was looking for an assistant to go over to his "other house" in Atlanta and open packages of paintings that he was shipping in, repack them and send them elsewhere per his instructions. It paid really well. Sounded good to me. I fell for the con, positive it was for real, taking the speed of his response as proof that someone *finally* saw me for the bonanza that I really am. I responded to the poster's email and sat back, breathing a sigh of relief that the long, hard hunt was over. After a few hours I rebooted my brain and tuned into those nagging little buzzers that had been going 'aangh, aangh" in the back of my mind. I called a couple of friends, both of whom informed me that hitting the delete button on any response from Oz was not optional if I wanted to stay out of the federal pen. The odds that this guy was not planning to use me as a mule to smuggle drugs or some other illegal contraband or at the very least launder money were slim to none, so time to move on.

And I did trudge on, my responses to Craigslist opportunities going from "I am a former lawyer, looking for part time work using my management and organizational skills" to "Please don't throw my resume out when you see that I used to practice law," figuring that maybe refreshing candor would get me what straightforward business drudge hadn't. Nothing worked. I got no responses that did not involve sex, drugs or fraud. Overcome with frustration, I took myself to lunch and drafted an open letter from my friends to the public, to be published in an alternative newspaper, beseeching the readers to find a job for their friend. I never published it, but I kept it in reserve. I'm sure my friends wouldn't have minded; they would have done it themselves if they'd thought of it.

Continuing to flail about, I decided to start a business, proofreading and editing for students applying for jobs or schools. I thought my pitch was clever:

I can't cook but I can write! Working with a good writer is like telling a cook that you want your hamburger medium with a little pink in the middle. You can't cook it that way yourself (at least I can't), but you can explain what you want and the cook knows how to make a perfect burger for you. I do the same thing with your thoughts—I edit your job cover letters and school applications to say what you want and to make your voice heard above the crowd.

And so on, listing my hours and fees and payment instructions. I put my ad on Craigslist and quickly got a job, so exciting, a nice young woman applying for graduate school. Her $90 payment helped defray the $180 I had spent frantically reserving domain names on Godaddy.com, such gems as bettaletta.com, letterbiz.com, intowords.com werdplace.com, werdsmith.com, thelastwerd.com, n2words.com, in2words.com, optimumwriter. com and wordheifer.com (named for the word that caused my father to come in second in his grammar school spelling bee).

I rode high on the strength of that first gig, patiently reposting on Craigslist every two days so as not to be flagged as a spammer. Time went on and nothing happened, then more nothing, then an email. I opened it eagerly: "You moron, do you really think anyone wants to read this drivel??

I have flagged you and you better stop posting immediately!" I was both incensed and deflated; it had taken a lot of energy and self motivation to keep changing the posts just enough to get past the censors every few days. If this was the thanks I was going to get for my ingenuity, I would take my business elsewhere. "Elsewhere" turned out to be an immediately defunct website whose design parted me from another $350. So much for entrepreneurship.

Finally an opportunity did come my way, one that seemed exciting: an interview at the High Museum of Art. Ever since I had seen the posting six weeks previously, I had been obsessing over this job, convinced that it was the only job left for me in town. It sounded like a good job—a reputable employer, part-time, dealing with speakers and artists, doing non-stressful administrative work like booking airfares and hotels, no foreign drug czars in sight. This was right up my alley, in the art world, where I felt a great deal of passion and enthusiasm, a refreshing change from the listless days of the recent past, waking up daily to the job of looking for a job.

I worked hard to get the interview, pulled out all the stops, including calls to the Director of the Museum and the Chairman of the Board. Interesting times when a fifty-six-year-old lawyer and businesswoman has to call in those kinds of markers for a $15/hour part-time job as an administrative assistant. I worried and worried over the interview; how was I going to convince my interviewer that I was the perfect person for this job? Because I felt that this was it, I absolutely had to get this job, put an end to getting up in the morning for no reason at all, supporting myself out of dwindling cash reserves. There was no other option and there was no other possible outcome. I was going to get this job.

The interview started: two people, not one, head and associate head of the education department, both very nice women. I knew I was going to have to persuade them that I wasn't overqualified, and I was prepared for that. I was not prepared for a deal breaker from the outset—my unfamiliarity with the PowerPoint software program. I figured that my willingness to take a quickie course in the program would carry the day. Not so. I started pedaling my strengths harder and harder, without any visible forward momentum, like my recent experience at the swimming pool when my son bet me that I couldn't make it from one end to the other underwater. I had gained weight at the time and was extraordinarily buoyant as a result. Though I started on the bottom of the pool taking long and (I thought) powerful strokes, I kept floating to the surface, ending up more or less in the same spot that I had begun. My protestations met by my interviewers' dubious responses had the same painfully static quality.

To hammer the next nail in, my interviewers asked whether I knew how to run an old-fashioned carousel slide show. I started sweating. Yeah, sure, I knew how to run one, and the odds of my doing it right under pressure were slim. I had memories of fighting with the slides, making double sure they were inserted correctly only to have the images come on backwards or upside down or the slides pop clean out of the carousel onto the floor. I soldiered on anyway, assuring them that I was solidly competent, telling the part of my brain that was sending up flares to can it.

The part of my brain that wanted to can the interview is where logic and reason reside, and while it has some patience for the folly that on occasion emanates from neighboring regions, its patience has limits. It sat still for the interview dialogue for a few more minutes, then it raised its hand and said, "I'm now part of this conversation and the answer is no." It continued, showing a disloyal affinity for my Craigslist detractor: "You must be an idiot. You can't go to work full time at a law firm because it's too stressful but you can prostrate yourself for a job that has you sweating in the interview because you *know* you'll screw it up? Are you that stupid? Well, you may be, but I'm not. This job is not for you."

Suzy shot back, "You shut the fuck up. Are you going to pay the bills? I'll be really careful with the carousel trays and I'll get all the PowerPoint slides right and figure out what cables go where, and whether the speaker has Mac PowerPoint or PC PowerPoint and convert all the slides an hour before the event when they bring the wrong thing and do whatever else they tell me to. This is do or die here and you stay out of it."

My internal conversation continued in this vein for a while, as my mouth and some lingering part of my brain responded to questions posed by my interviewers and made what I hoped was urbane small talk. There came a time when I created a little space in my brain off to the side and a bunch of us talked about whether it was time to call bullshit on this. We all knew these women weren't going to hire me, the women knew they weren't going to hire me, and all that was left was for Suzy to let go.

She put up a good fight, but she finally gave in, opening the door for me to be straightforward: "I can tell that you have concerns about whether I am right for this job and that you particularly want someone who already has a background in PowerPoint." They perked up a little. I continued: "Maybe you'll interview twenty-five more people and I'll still be the most qualified for the job, who knows? In that case you'll hire me and everything will be great. But I doubt it, so I'll tell you what, if you come across a job that seems more suitable for me, please keep me in mind."

They appeared grateful, released from the uncomfortable choice between telling me "no" outright or letting me go on my way thinking I was under consideration when I wasn't. We all relaxed, chatted for a few minutes about nothing in particular and parted, with me feeling oddly content.

My cousin, Erin, was shocked at my demeanor when I told her ruefully but with reasonable good humor that I had not gotten the job. She said she thought I'd be curled up in a ball on the floor somewhere, catatonic, because she knew how much I had counted on getting the job and what a disappointment it must have been to be turned down. She had a point, so why did I feel okay?

Given my history, my little theatrical revue in the middle of the interview had been wonderfully satisfying. I had been aware of all the different players (mine and theirs), all of my different feelings and all of my different thoughts simultaneously, and it was enormously rewarding to synthesize it all and come up with an answer on the spot that was true and right. This from a woman who started therapy twenty-nine years ago having to learn, painstakingly, step by step, how to even identify feelings other than fear, whose roadmap I carried with me at all times, much less act on them in real time.

At the ripe age of twenty-eight, I literally had no idea what the other feelings were, what they felt like or what they meant. I had been shut down at such an early age, I missed all that stuff entirely.

Year one of my therapy was spent building my repertoire, putting on the labels. Year two was for developing my response options (get mad, talk about it, walk away, all the stuff that's automatic with most people). Year three was dedicated to shortening up my response time. With anything that was subtle or called for major confrontation on my part, it initially took me about a week. First I had to figure out, spurred by some nagging sensation or a desire to binge eat, that somebody had said or done something that had bothered me. Then I had to figure out who and what it was, pinpoint what I felt, look at what my choices were and, finally, have a conversation with the other person. This used to drive my children batshit; they had moved on to the next thing five seconds later and would literally vibrate with frustration when a week later I would come back to rehash what seemed to them ancient history.

I have only ever met one other person with this experience of himself, the unlikeliest person. He was with me as an outpatient at Alexander Hospital, looked like a mountain man, in overalls with a long gray beard. He didn't talk much, but when he asked one particular question in a group meeting a light bulb went off in my head, and I asked him if things worked the same way for him as they did for me. They did, so then we both knew that there were at least two of us.

CHAPTER THIRTY-ONE

THE HOLIDAYS

T HEY SAY THAT THE HOLIDAYS are hard for
everyone, that those of us who are emotionally
challenged shouldn't feel like we are the only
ones. I don't know about that; it sure looked like
fun from the outside—nice, functional families
getting together, cooking and eating and opening
presents. I'd had that at times during my marriage,
and I knew what it felt like; it felt good, and the
lack of it, quite naturally, did not.

Still, despite being on my own and away from
my children, I thought that I had achieved a

certain stability by the winter of 2010, so when Christmas approached, I figured that I would be fine. That turned out to be overly optimistic, and in fact I made a little side trip back to the "other place" during that holiday season of 2010. Nothing too intense, just a brief visit to the world where shapes and their purposes were elusive: keys might be for carving turkeys, pens might serve to open doors, and the fog fell and lifted in waves. Twice I walked into the Atlanta airport, all the way through Security and to the transit train before I realized that I had no idea what gate I was going to. Once I checked into the wrong terminal and presented my baggage claim stub as a boarding pass. I made more than one illegal u-turn and perhaps drove the wrong way down a one-way street (of that I had only a hazy recollection but I was pretty sure it happened).

It reminded me of the feeling that I had had in the days immediately before, during and after my hospitalizations, and that was a feeling that I had hoped never to experience again. "The world is too much with us" is the refrain that looped through my mind. I am not a poet and I never understood any but the simplest, most direct poetry—Edgar Allan Poe was the limit of my comfort zone. I doubt that I had read that Wordsworth line since I first saw it in high school forty years earlier, but it stuck with me, because even as a teenager that line resonated. I later learned from researching it on

the internet what the line was supposed to mean—
that the materialism of the world played too great
a role in shaping our lives and our destinies—but it
captured something different for me: a weariness, a
state of feeling constantly overwhelmed, a burden
carried too long that begged to be lifted.

Life seemed more painful than I was in the
mood for, although there were interludes of
genuine delight and merriment during those
holidays, principally revolving around my daughter,
Juliana's, twenty-first birthday. Her pleasure at,
among other things, finally being "legal," brought
back fond memories of my own good times and
escapades. I remember thinking, "My God, how
do we ever lose our way from being that happy,
from feeling that loved, looking forward so eagerly
to the next day and the one to follow?" That was
not a rhetorical question, and I actually knew the
answer: start a landslide, and you are likely to end
up on the bottom of the hill under a pile of debris,
unless you know how to stop your descent. At that
time, I did not.

So the uplifting interlude with Juliana was
brief, and I quickly sank further into a familiar mix
of apathy, anxiety and depression. Then, a week
after Juliana's birthday celebration, I heard that I
had lost a friend, a good friend, to a sudden and
untimely death, and that knocked me sideways.
I had long understood that I didn't choose the
people I connected with—my family who weren't

blood relatives—it just happened, and that had been the case with Ted and his wife, Elaine. They were my neighbors for three years beginning in 2005, but I only knew them for two, having spent the first year after I moved into the house in hiding, traumatized by post-divorce aftershocks. Ted was a very outgoing person and after taking in the unusual sight of my cat, Horace, going on walks with me and my dog, Henrietta, he made friends with me and drew me out. We grew to be so close that I trusted him and Elaine with the information that I was going into the hospital in the summer of 2008, and that Henrietta and Horace would be walked every day by a pet service. They offered to check on things, and when three weeks in the hospital turned into ten, Ted, who was extremely handy, watched over my place and took care of anything that needed to be fixed. When I moved out of town in 2009, Ted placed a sign in the newly poured cement sidewalk commemorating the "Horace Memorial Highway," where my cat used to take his neighborhood strolls. Ted had a superb sense of humor as well as being kind, gentle, and a person of honor. I also appreciated that he got a kick out of the Suzy side of me, fascinated that someone who seemed so bright could sometimes be so clueless.

When I called Elaine to say that I had dropped into town for a visit, I launched into my usual banter, faltering only when I picked up a strange tone in her voice. "Elaine, what's wrong?" I asked. "Did Ginger die?" (Their beloved terrier had been on the way out for months.) "No, it's Ted." "What about him?" "He's dead, he died of a heart attack six weeks ago."

I was driving at the time and had to pull over. I had always been extremely lucky in losing very few friends or family to untimely deaths, so I was ill prepared for this, had no coping mechanism in place for the shock and the pain of it. I tried to visit Elaine, but she wasn't home and I stopped in at another neighbor's. I burst into tears, and a box of Kleenex later, I left his house to go sit on a bench by the water nearby. I cried and then cried some more. Finally I was able to visit Elaine in the late afternoon and we had a good visit, laughing over memories of Ted and crying some, too. By this time I was mostly cried out, so I was able to be relatively strong and composed for Elaine. I knew that this was expected of me, and it is a practice that I understood conceptually but have always found difficult to execute, because if I am feeling the impulse to cry, I can bite my tongue, command myself not to cry, dig a nail into my palm and think about all the calm ocean vistas in the world, but nothing is going to keep back the tears. At any rate, I held myself together during our visit but came unglued again after, because I had lost someone I could count on, a true friend, and I did then and do now hold tightly to every jewel in that crown.

The good news was that I rebounded fairly quickly, both from the general holiday malaise and from the news about Ted. I went back to work after the holidays were over, and that helped. Therapy sessions resumed, and that helped, too. More than that, though, I sensed that by dint of all of the efforts of the preceding two and a half years, I had regained a measure of my former resiliency. Considering that I was only six months out of the hospital at Alexander, that boded well, but I knew that the process of recovery is long, and I was but a step on the way.

CHAPTER THIRTY-TWO

BRUISED AND BLOODIED, BUT UNBOWED

DID I SAY THAT THE PROCESS OF RECOVERY is long? I didn't mean long, I meant LONG, as in years, not days, weeks or months. I remember being incensed when Dr. Finster at Farraday opined in his initial written assessment of my condition, three weeks into the program, that my chances for recovery were "fair to good with ongoing intensive treatment." The words leapt off the page of his report, stunning me, striking me, blinding me like a flare aimed straight at my eyes.

"Fair to good," was he kidding? That was it? My hope for a near term future that resembled my blithe, not-too-distant "southern belle/ lawyer/ responsible mother" past reduced to ashes with seven words? There I was at a top notch hospital, staying for weeks, ten as it turned out; how was it possible that the resident expert couldn't assure me that I would be sailing around like my old self in no time? I accosted him, harangued him, and came away with the unsatisfying admission that he tended to err on the side of being conservative, which did little to allay my fury and disbelief.

"Ongoing intensive treatment" indeed! What did that even mean? My doctor's idea, as it turned out, was therapy three to four times a week. I never for a minute took him seriously, since I had neither the resources nor the inclination for that kind of commitment to an ongoing therapeutic program. I decided that individual therapy sessions once a week backed up by monthly visits to a psychopharmacologist were gracious plenty, and upon my release from Farraday, that is exactly what I set up.

Only after I ended up back in the hospital a scant seventeen months later, at Alexander, did I recall the advice that I had been given at Farraday and begin to wonder whether I had ignored it at my peril. Even so, it was grudgingly that I upped my therapy from once to twice a week, and added a group session on top of the monthly visits to check on my medication. My stubbornness may seem stupid until you think about it—when you have worked and worked at something with seemingly little to show for it, the last thing you want to hear is that the single solution to your problem is to work harder. But while part of me still balked, part of me also understood that I had been beyond naïve to think that that the road back from where I'd gone would take anything less than extreme commitment, patience, work and more work. And that sometimes the best it would ever get would be a flatline where everything was okay but not great. Neither would everything be miserable all of the time and sometimes, with increasing frequency as the months went by, I would feel like I used to feel, easy and natural, with the ability to laugh freely and maintain a modicum of stability and peace.

Good call on my part. I knew from my face when I looked in the mirror some time after I checked out of Alexander, after a few months of more concentrated therapy, that my "set point" was higher, meaning that I was farther along the road to recovery. I didn't look drawn, tight, closed in, worried, tense and preoccupied anymore, at least not most of the time. I was still more introspective than most people, and I knew that I might always live in my head to a greater degree than might be optimally healthy. My stock answer for years when people got frustrated with how unobservant and preoccupied I tended to be was, "Yes, but I have a rich interior life."

At times my disposition was positively sunny, and that was hard to believe, because despite all of the progress, I realized that there was still no amount of reassurance, no quantity of expressions of love, no number of blatant, flat out "I love you's," that had yet convinced me that I was loved, cared for, cherished and approved of in a way that satisfied my needs. I went to Virginia to visit my three children one time during this period, a whirlwind three-day trip, three cities in as many days, and at the end of the trip I counted the number of people I had been with or with whom I had spoken at length who cared about me. These were people who I *knew* cared about me strongly and deeply and the affection and depth of feeling was returned. It was twenty-six people, and that didn't count the additional people with whom I had had brief contact who I knew also bore me extreme good will.

It wasn't enough.

For a long time, I saved the messages from people in my cell phone, particularly from my children, that said "I love you" or "Have a safe trip" or "I really enjoyed the visit." I was constantly having to decide which messages to delete because my message box was full of one-liners that were casual expressions of love and regard from the senders but lifelines for me.

The saved messages were not enough.

I found that I had something in common with the younger generation who text and "bbm" and iChat and facebook and tweet 24/7. I checked my cell phone for voice messages and texts constantly, my email as well, on a ridiculously frequent basis. I don't know if we all were doing it for the same reason: mine was that I didn't feel safe unless I saw a concrete expression that someone felt connected to me. It was the reflection of love that comforted me for a moment, just a moment, and then I felt cast out again, until the next communication came.

I went to Sunday morning services and listened hard to the message of the love felt for me by God, or the Universe, or the Universal Mind, or the Supreme Intelligence or whatever other nomenclature was currently in vogue for the Divine, and I worked really hard to get it, to take in that there was no other answer for someone like me, that I would only find peace and comfort if I allowed that message to find a home in me. But I could not, not yet; something stopped me, saying, "No, you don't belong here."

As it turned out, the first big turning point, the first and for a time the only thing to fill the gaping wound, was purpose, specifically the purpose filled by writing this book. It quite possibly kept me alive, certainly kept despair at bay as it nibbled around my midsection. The turning point was unexpected: I didn't plan to write a book, I didn't try to be funny, and when I gave it, partially completed, to a few friends to read, I did it because I wanted them to understand what I had been through, not to comment on my literary capabilities. But they did, first one, then two, then a lot of people, and they told me that what I had written was good, really good. Then a writer friend told me, "You don't need a psychiatrist, you need a literary agent."

That thought had never occurred to me, but once broached the idea gripped me. I started thinking that I was a good writer, and it became something to hold on to, something that no one and nothing could take away. If I died tomorrow, I would know that I had written something that had worth, that measured up. What a turnaround, when so much of my life and world to that point had been viewed through a lens of insecurity and doubt.

After the fulfillment of writing this book started to take hold, other lifelines began to appear, all of them intangible but nonetheless critical, all of them addressing what ailed me in perfect symmetry: willingness, acceptance, mindfulness, patience and compassion for myself. The same fixes that had been presented to me by all and sundry in the alternative community for years and, more recently, even by the mainstream world, only I had consistently rejected them all because I wanted a magic pill, needed that pill, would not, could not, conceive of dealing with the pain that I felt without it. I searched for that magic pill for years, suffering through tests and more tests, dosing and re-dosing, calibrations and combinations, side effects and no effects, hoping, always hoping, only to be informed on multiple occasions that I was "medication resistant," that, for me, hard work was my only solution, that the doctors had nothing more to offer me and I was on my own. Although at Alexander I had begun to consider the possibility that there was no drug that could help me, I still refused to accept that result with any degree of finality, and continued to go from doctor to doctor, clinic to clinic, categorically rejecting that such a diagnosis could be true, in fact was true. I could not accept that, live or die, happy or unhappy, my condition was going to be of my own making, that tools and props would be available, principally a good therapist, but it was going to be up to me, Self-Determination 101. Not possible.

Until in 2011 I was tipped over the edge on what turned out to be my penultimate visit to my psychiatrist, Dr. Hathaway, the latest doctor responsible for supervising my by then virtually non-existent medication. Dr. Hathaway was out of town, but the new resident assigned to my case was there, as well as a covering psychiatrist. After interviewing me on her own for some minutes, the resident began reading from my chart in order to brief the covering physician. She began: "The patient is not currently taking any psychiatric medication. She has been diagnosed with borderline personality disorder. . . ." Whoops! There we were in that alternative universe that so many of my therapists seemed to inhabit. I cut the resident off in mid-sentence since, of all of the diagnoses ever applied to me, borderline personality disorder was not one, nor, according to a swift consultation with my regular therapist and my own not insignificant learning on the subject, should it have been. I was outraged, and took the matter up with Dr. Hathaway in absentia via a furious exchange of emails. He apologized, acknowledged the shortcomings of labels and we left a fuller discussion for his return.

However, by the time Dr. Hathaway was back in the office and I came in for my next, and likely to be final, appointment, not only had I lost interest in his opinion or that of his resident, I no longer cared what any other psychiatrist or for that matter any other individual on the planet had to say on the subject. I had finally had enough and, pushed to the limit, did what I should have done years ago: I made up my own mind about what was wrong with me, what could be done about it and who could do it.

I proffered my self-assessment to Dr. Hathaway, that there was no pill that was going to make me feel better, not even a little bit, because I suffered from bouts of despair, not depression, and there is no pill for despair. I suffered from an ongoing existential crisis, and there is no pill for that. Or for visceral fears of abandonment. Or low self-esteem. It all seemed obvious when you looked at it the right way. Of all my therapists, Dr. Renway's assessment that I had no diagnosable disorder and suffered mostly from emotional disregulation had come closest to the truth, but still no cigar. Maybe I would have understood it if she had explained her thoughts on my condition to me in plain English.

Not only did Dr. Hathaway agree that medication was not going to help me, he added some interesting input. In his opinion, in an effort to de-stigmatize psychiatric disorders, the medical profession had over-promoted the efficacy of medication, the logic being that if you responded to medication, then you were sick just like someone with the flu, hence no stigma. The campaign worked pretty well on that score, but played hell with people like me, seducing us with pipedreams of magic pills that for us would never materialize.

Coincidentally, if you believe in coincidences, six days after my visit to Dr. Hathaway, an article appeared on the front page of *The New York Times* titled "Talk Doesn't Pay, So Psychiatry Turns Instead to Drug Therapy."[9] The point of the article was that in the current world, the doctor who prescribes your psychiatric medication is no longer a person who knows anything about what makes you tick, nor can he afford to care. It's all about the drugs, because at current insurance reimbursement levels, he or she can earn $150 for three fifteen-minute meds visits as opposed to $90 for a talk therapy session of equal length.

So, the pieces started to fall into place, though I can't blame the medical community for my predicament. (I suppose that you can call twenty-nine years of fruitless drug experimentation a predicament.) Even though no one went so far as to say that there was no medication at all that could help me, it was suggested more than once that there was no one solution for me, no one pill. I just couldn't bear to accept it. Until, finally, I could no longer dodge what my own experience was telling me, and I acknowledged that it was possible, and then probable, and then true, a hard truth that I had fought against for more years than I could count, because I never believed that I could help myself, never believed that I had a choice in whether or not to be sick.

The movie *A Beautiful Mind*—that was a unique situation, a schizophrenic able to disregard his delusions; that wasn't me, or so I thought. Only it *was* me, it was and is the exact model that I have to follow, the only way through the darkness that I believe will work for me. I have to choose, sometimes every day, sometimes every hour, whether I want to be sick or well. Once I have chosen to be well, I have to discipline my mind to support that choice, consciously confronting and re-directing contrary thinking. Having accepted that my recovery depends on this discipline, it isn't as impossible as I thought it would be; the bar is high but not unattainable.

And lucky for me, today there are any number of teachings that I can call on for help. There is a spiritual movement called "New Thought" which adopts as a core tenet the premise that how we choose to think creates our personal experiences. They have services every Sunday. I go. Cognitive therapy, developed in the 1960s, also focuses on thought as the route to recovery and is widely practiced today. I follow it. These avenues to recovery suit me, just as other paths, like the AA model of faith-based action ("fake it 'til you make it") have suited millions of others. Whatever works.

I have been off all medication except a mild sleep aid for two years now. I don't miss it, especially the side effects. I don't miss the head trip, waiting and hoping while we "adjusted my meds," titrating up, titrating down, mixing, adding and subtracting over and over and over again. While it is occasionally an art, this is no science, and most often in my experience, it is merely throwing darts at a dart board, blindfolded. I have withdrawn myself from the game.

Which doesn't mean that I don't have to confront the scorpion in me from time to time, but that part of me is less active, less entrenched, and I get the idea that she's planning on retiring soon and spending her winters in Florida and cruising in the Caribbean. Bon voyage.

PART FIVE

RUN FOR THE ROSES

CHAPTER THIRTY-THREE

PATIENCE

ONE OF THE THINGS that I still have a hard time with is patience and accepting that not everything happens on my schedule, no matter how much I want it to and how much I try to control things. I would have killed to get work as an editor when I launched my editing business, writingchallenged.com. I would have done anything. I was pathetically grateful for the one client I got before Craigslist shut down my advertising efforts and I gave up on the business. Once I got hired as a contract lawyer a few months later, I forgot all about it, except that I retained a certain conceptual fondness that prompted me to leave the name as part of the message on my voice mail ("Hi, you have reached writingchallenged. com"), giving rise to much confusion on the part of innocent callers.

Ten months later, still working as a contract lawyer and into my third round of interviews for a permanent position at my current law firm, I got an email from a friend: "My friend needs help editing a piece, I'll put you two in touch." I was buried at work, but what the hell. The piece came, with the request that I "imagine it, please, as an op-ed in the *Times*." Okay, fine, except that it wasn't even close; in fact it was an incomprehensible rant that had something to do with the technical non-existence of the internet. The author and I went back and forth with no result and finally I never heard from him again. No problem, chalk it up to experience. I wasn't interested anyway because I had enough other work.

One week later I left for Virginia to take care of Rachel while Leo went out of town. The night of my arrival I opened my email to find an urgent plea from my one and only real client, the one who had responded to my Craigslist ad months earlier— she had an emergency and needed help getting a paper written on the Benin tribe of Africa. She needed it by the next morning and it was already 9:00 p.m. I actually had studied the Benin in college as part of my art history major, so editing her paper wasn't as difficult as it sounds. I did my best, and thought, ok, that's weird, two in a week. Three days later she emailed me back with another request, again eleventh hour, but I couldn't do it. Not quite as surprising, this one I could chalk up to the needs of an ongoing client. Two days later, I got a phone message out of the blue from an old friend: his eighteen-year-old nephew was facing a three-year prison term, and the judge wanted him to write an essay about how thirty-six months in jail would change his life, and could I please edit his paper? Having served time at Alexander, this also wasn't as hard as it sounds. I also had become a devoted fan of *Break Out Kings*, a TV show in which the main characters are prisoners who are let out to help catch other criminals. The show includes prison scenes, so I had multi-level experience that I could bring to bear on this one. My friend said to just let him know how much time I spent and he would send me a check.

A check was already in the mail for the Benin paper and I think some money was coming in for my work on the failed op-ed piece. Gee, God, this would have been really nice when I was destitute and spending every waking hour trying to promote my business just to pay a fraction of my rent. Why was work finally dropping out of the sky when I already had a job and looked to be on the verge of getting another one, a really stable well-paying one at that? It wasn't like I had mentioned the business to another living soul for almost a year, so why now?

My takeaway was that it was a reminder to me that I cannot always cause things to happen on my own schedule, no matter how hard I try. It was like my efforts to add some sexual activity involving another human participant to my life. For months I had been devoting hours upon hours to this end, poring over eHarmony and JDate, with little to show for it, other than a very clear approximation of the number of male Sarah Palin devotees in my corner of the world and a brush with a potential murderer. The last man I had a date with I grabbed by the collar and demanded, "Don't you want to have fabulous sex at least one more time before you die?" Trust me, sex with a middle-aged woman who has been celibate for a while is virtually guaranteed to be fabulous, although I don't think a lot of men have figured that out yet, despite the recent "cougar" vogue.

Being in a semi-committed relationship, the object of my assault (did I say that? I meant of my affections) said that he had to give it some thought, plus he would prefer to be the one doing at least some of the courting. Fair enough, even though my personal opinion was that time was a wastin'. But this time, I actually could see the value of a timetable not of my devising. What I was getting from my elusive lover was much more valuable than sex. He liked me and I knew it, he thought that I was attractive and I knew it, and he was there for me as a friend and I knew it. He had read this book and he still liked me, still thought I was attractive and funny and smart. He said so more than once. And he didn't ditch me after he read my book; in fact he read it twice and made insightful comments. He didn't ditch me after I collared him at lunch. The mere existence of a man like this, one man on the face of the earth who knew who I was and still saw value in me as a person and as a woman, including but not limited to sexual attraction, gave bloom to a sense of self worth that I hadn't felt for a very long time. That was worth a lot more than any physical interlude.

This is one example of what recovery is for me, the knowledge and understanding that I can draw from my relationships with people the things that I never got, the sense of stability and belonging, and I can build my life as I go. It is the awareness that when life presents me with opportunities to enhance my sense of value, such as unexpected compliments and fortuitous events, not to overlook them but to recognize them and add whatever is presented to my storehouse. My recovery includes the full knowledge that I will still do foolish and unstable-seeming things from time to time—who doesn't? But I will not lose my balance irretrievably just because I did something that was less than perfect in my own or anybody else's eyes. I will be hurt by life's circumstances and I will feel pain, but the pendulum will not swing beyond the point of no return. I will have successes and triumphs that will feel like all of the promises that were ever made to me have been kept, and in the face of that I will hold a part of myself in check. I will be impatient that the world doesn't run on my clock and I nevertheless will take a deep breath and keep on going. I will hear the voice of my default inside my head in times of extreme stress or fear telling me, "I can't get through this without eating myself senseless," or "I want to kill myself," and I will dismiss the voice as the echo of the outdated program that it is and select another default. It is all as easy, and as hard, as that.

CHAPTER THIRTY-FOUR

WHAT A DIFFERENCE A YEAR CAN MAKE

E VENTS PROVED OUT my postulates of the
last chapter. Okay, I presented them as facts,
but they were really postulates at the time, a slight
deception. Exactly one year after my last day at
Alexander Hospital, I accepted a job at a prestigious
law firm that would make me solvent for the first
time in six years. Not only that, I had finally found a
job in law that was the perfect combination of top-
notch colleagues, camaraderie, work that didn't
exceed the boundaries of my understanding, a

schedule that conformed to a regular work week and a salary that not only allowed me to be self-supporting but also to feel good about myself. (It was hard to give up measuring my professional worth at least in part by dollars earned.)

Just that scant year before, while I was at Alexander, my brother was told to expect that I would never work again, and it was said in all seriousness by a very bright doctor based on his clinical evaluation of me. I decided that my recent success in obtaining a legal position was just one more proof of how inexact a science psychiatric diagnosis is and that you shouldn't believe everything you hear from even the most esteemed doctors, especially when it comes to knowing yourself.

From the spiritual side, getting that job was a miracle. From the human side, it took hard work, hope, faith, determination, and months of indefatigable work on the part of my friend, Sophie, the world's greatest living legal recruiter. One of my oldest friends gave me the highest compliment when I told her about the new job: "You have true grit," she said. Of all the reactions to the news of my job, all of the excitement from other friends and family, that was the one that lit me up. Yes, I had gotten a great job in the face of a bad economy, and at an age when it can be hard to find work (I was then fifty-seven years old). That was something to be proud of, without a doubt. But that didn't come close to the satisfaction of knowing that I had clawed my way out of the muck, struggled to my knees and finally stood up on my own two feet, solidly planted on the ground, unwavering. Maybe people who haven't been through a decline of the magnitude that mine achieved can't begin to understand, and there is probably a desire on the part of some to pretend that the implosions of my past hadn't occurred, that they were just a little glitch, that's all, and now look at her, why she's just fine, isn't she? For my part, I don't want to sweep any part of that journey under the rug: I want to celebrate it like I've never celebrated anything in my life. It is my crowning achievement; I can't imagine surpassing it and wouldn't want to if the opportunity presented itself. (Let's see, should I collapse again to see if I can drag myself upright one more time?)

And the job was not the only thing that had turned around. I received the offer while I was in Italy on vacation with my daughter, Juliana. It was the trip of a lifetime and we re-bonded on a scale that I never could have imagined. For the most part we agreed automatically on where to go and where to eat, and both enjoyed sightseeing, sunbathing and adventurous side trips in equal measure. Juliana was in such raptures over the food that she photographed most of her meals for posterity (i.c., Facebook, which serves as posterity for her generation). It was an uncanny replay of the pleasurable trips I had shared with my parents, but for me and Juliana our renewed bond signaled not an oasis in the desert, but a re-establishment of the old order when we had shared a typical mother-daughter rapport, easy and comfortable, with a dash of conflict. To have regained that bond with Juliana was a pearl beyond price.

Yes, my stock was definitely up: I couldn't miss a traffic light, the trains in Italy ran on time just for me, everybody showed up when they said they would, day after day, and not one but two law firms had courted me like I was the #1 NFL draft choice. Most times I was at ease, and my thoughts were clear and unencumbered.

The change in me was that I was mostly able to bask in my happiness, savor that time in full knowledge that it was a fleeting moment, because changes would come, I knew it, and not all of them would be as buoyant as my present circumstances. I was right—soon afterwards, I had a major flea infestation and a minor flood in my apartment, Rachel came for the summer and then was gone, my dog, Henrietta, had to have a kidney removed, and dating became tedious and disappointing. So what? Let Mrs. Kellogg from eleventh grade ask me again whether I would merely survive or whether I would prevail. This time I didn't care what her answer was, I knew mine.

CHAPTER THIRTY-FIVE

HOMAGE TO MY MOTHER
OR THE FAT LADY SINGS

FOR MOST OF MY LIFE, my relationship with my mother was conflicted, to say the least. At moments I disliked her, disapproved of her priorities. (Yes, Tao Master, I not only refused to detach from my judgments, in this particular arena I positively clung to them.) I reacted to her violently. I lay in wait for her, for moments when I could catch her in a behavior of which I disapproved, to confirm to myself that she still deserved my contempt. The moments came often enough that I didn't usually have to question my *bona fides*.

Like the time in the Spring of 2011 when my mother was in the car, directing her nurse/hip-surgery recovery assistant on the route to take to drive me home from a colonoscopy. I was in the back seat, all too quickly recovered from the disappointingly unopiate-like drug that they had given me to knock me out. In the space of a few minutes and a couple of miles, this was the conversation. My mother: "There you've got a stop sign. Now you can go. You want the right lane and you can turn right if that car over there will go. COME ON DUMMY! He's from out of town, so he doesn't know he can go right on red." Ruby: "Do you think he might be going straight?" "He's not going straight, there's nothing down there, unless he's going to those empty apartments. He's not going there. . . . You were right, Ruby, he's going straight. Get in the right lane. Oh look at this, maybe we'll make the light! Uh-oh. Can you get in the left lane? Now go!"

Okay, I thought at the time, so she's controlling, she's vain, manipulative, perfectionistic and arrogant. For many years she was extremely volatile, exhibiting rages that left me in tatters. Her outlook on food, diet and looks had carved out canyons deep in my psyche. The question was, where did all of that leave me now, decades later, still smarting over insults, real and imagined? The answer to that, surprisingly, would change dramatically for the better in her eighty-fifth and my fifty-sixth years of life.

This book started out as a blog, but it never attracted many followers—three friends and one stranger in six months. My experiences at Alexander Hospital seemed to require that I write about them; there really wasn't much choice in the matter. The words came of their own accord, flowed out of my brain, down my arms, through my fingers and onto the page. For some reason, flinging my thoughts into cyberspace encouraged the flow, so I chose blogging as a medium.

At first I used the blog to try desperately to connect with others who had shared my kind of mental distress, but it never happened. (I did find two riotous blogs along the way, *we are respectable negroes* and *the bitchy waiter*, so the effort was worth it.) I also gave the blog address to my mother and my brother early on as a last ditch effort to make myself visible to them in a way that mattered to me. Judging by the lack of response from either of them, it didn't work, but it was worth a try.

After a while I came to look upon the blog as a personal journal, a creative, cathartic exercise, one that I was proud of because, as I re-read it, I thought that certain passages were pleasingly expressive, even witty, clever and poignant, and that made me happy. I have such an accomplished family and was feeling like such a failure, that my writing gave me back a measure of pride, of self-confidence.

As my outrage at events that I witnessed and experienced as a hapless guest at Alexander began to wane, I started to write about my life in general—my dog, my cat, looking for a job and, with great and obvious gusto, my mother. While she had taken a few hits in the early going, I started lobbing the grenades at her for real when she went in for hip surgery on May 27, 2010.

On that day, in my mother's hospital room, I wrote a few lines that crossed into territory that most people would probably look upon as, "I can think it, but I'd never say it out loud, much less put it down on paper." I, of course, not only put it on paper, but put it in the blog, albeit a blog that was garnering as much attention as the Book of Nahum (revealed by answers.yahoo.com to be the least read book in the Bible, a fact which I find most interesting). I wrote:

My mother had hip replacement surgery in May of 2010, right after I was discharged from Alexander for good. I wanted her to come out of the surgery changed, subdued, older and weaker. No such luck. At eighty-five she sailed through it like a teenager. So I still was going to have to fight for my space at the trough, against a hog that not only was much older and more cunning than I, but soon no longer to be distracted by a bad hip. It was like pitting Red Riding Hood against a combination of Prince Machiavelli and The Terminator, hardly a fair fight, and I wasn't sure that I had the stamina for it.

So, how do you really feel about your mother?

Trick question, and the only answer that I knew consistently, without a shred of doubt, across all of the space and time that had made up my life to that point, was "strongly." Some time after I wrote that passage, I took it off the blog, recognizing its excess for what it was, an exorcism of some very unpleasant, yet visceral, feelings. I soon became aware, however, that I was living on borrowed time before someone either told my mother about that and other less than flattering passages in the blog or brought her a copy of them to read. I figured that I had better take matters into my own hands, so I asked my mother whether she had read my blog since the early days, on the off chance that her mind had been taken over by Ghandi and she had read it and not been disturbed. No such luck, so I gave it to her to read, with a great deal of trepidation and knowing that there was even a possibility that she would become furious and cut me out of her world.

I don't know about anyone else, but one of my favorite things about life is the curve balls. The times when you think you know what is going to happen, but it doesn't turn out at all the way you expected, and as the experience unfolds you get a glimpse of what exists at the juncture of fate, caprice, nature, nurture, science, psychology and whatever other forces you believe are at play in the world. I never feel more alive than at those times,

times that I know are going to be essential to the story of my life, not the window dressing, and that's how I felt as I waited for my mother's response.

As it turned out, she responded calmly, and while most of the words we exchanged escape me, I remember a sense of release and relief, and I remember her saying that I could ask her anything, that she had no secrets. Well, that was a switch. There had been nothing but secrets from my point of view for as long as I had been alive, but hey, I've refined the practice of turning on someone else's dime into something close to an art form, so I took this one right in stride, happy to get the news.

As time went by, and my mother continued to exhibit, without drama, a consistent demeanor of sympathy and support toward me, I began to revise my thinking about her and to review our history through a different lens. Because if you go back to the story of the car ride back from my colonoscopy, who was in the car? My mother. Who took me in, no questions asked, at the tender age of fifty-six, twice in fifteen months? My mother. Who was prepared to support me financially? My mother. Who was and is the best nurse on the planet if you are sick? My mother. This was an unexpected but dominant aspect of her personality for my entire life, and indeed it is shocking that I did not become a hypochondriac in order to elicit those ministrations on a continuing basis.

Who taught herself gardening (flower and vegetable), antique furniture and porcelains (English, Continental, American, Chinese, you name it), history, contemporary Chinese politics in the era of Mao, art (traditional and contemporary), haute cuisine (cooking and eating), connoisseurship of fine wines and haute couture? My mother. She read voraciously, and she read books of great depth along with the Victorian romances of my youth and Barbara Cartland paperbacks. *The Decline and Fall of the Roman Empire* was in our library and I am pretty sure that she had read it, or at least part of it. I remember her reading and talking about the atrocities of the Cultural Revolution in China in the '60s, and my being curious about what she was talking about, but not feeling comfortable enough to invade what seemed her private world of knowledge.

Who said to me when I was still living in Virginia and doing poorly that if I needed her to come to me that she would come "if I have to crawl up the steps to your house"—at a time when one of her hips and a knee were compromised and extremely painful, making it hard for her even to walk? My mother. Who announced, microphone in hand, at a 2009 luncheon for 100 loving mothers and daughters, that she was going to shock the group by telling them that, unlike the other mothers, she had been a bad mother, that she had quashed me at every turn and persistently opposed my efforts to become my own person? My mother.

And, reluctantly, I had to admit that my mother was physically beautiful, a stunning, imposing woman, not petite, but with broad shoulders, long legs and thick, dark brunette hair. She was often mistaken for Rosalind Russell on our travels, and that is a fair description, at least in terms of the pictures I have seen of the actress in the 1940s. I was with my mother once as a teenager, at a midnight dinner after a bullfight in Madrid, and a woman came up and asked for my mother's autograph, mistaking her for Ms. Russell. My mother complied, but signed her own name. More than physical beauty, my mother had a commanding presence, still has it in her 80s.

All told, I realized, this is not an insubstantial person, and to the extent that I have substance, it comes from her. She is a complicated person, and to the extent that I have depth and breadth, it comes from her. She is an enormously determined and courageous person, and to some extent, my own determination in the face of my personal devils comes from her. (The rest is Suzy's unique brand of quirky tenacity coming to the rescue.)

To the extent that I have strength, it comes from her. I watched her carry my father on her back for the last two years of his life, and that was a sight to behold—I've never seen anything like it and I expect that I never will. During that time, he was somewhere along the spectrum of dementia, but more than that, he was depressed, had all but given up. Golf, the great diversion of his lifetime, was beyond his capabilities. He had been fired from his volunteer work because he wouldn't learn how to use a computer. He couldn't drive anymore, couldn't see very well, couldn't hear well at all, and these things weighed heavily on him. When you asked him what he was doing, he would say, "Sleeping the day away, what does it look like?" And that's mostly what he did, nap and doze, nap and doze.

I would have been oh so tempted to let him drift away. My mother was made of sterner stuff. She gave him chores, she took him out to lunch, she took him out to dinner, she pushed him hard and then she pushed him harder. When he slacked off, she would roar at him, "You're not trying! Now look at me, here's how you do it!" And she would show him how to push himself up from his chair or how to bend and pick up a dog toy or put on a sock. It wasn't about being kind; there was nothing kind about it in its day-to-day operation, and I once heard him say to her, "I wouldn't talk to a dog the way you talk to me." It was at once painful to watch and awe-inspiring—I don't think I could have done it. I think the necessary cruelty of it would have been beyond me, but I think that she stole hours out of the mouth of oblivion for him, and I think she did it for him, not for herself.

My mother also has positive qualities that I lack, that I respect, that I could learn from. As impatient as she may be in the more mundane of life's situations (such as road traffic as encountered with me and Ruby), she has rare patience in more serious settings. Like with me. Prior to The Talk About The Blog, she had been waiting me out, for months on end. I used to watch her do it and marvel at how absolutely constant she remained in her approach to me, her smiles, her endearments, her pleasant requests. Her voice held delight when she heard that it was me at the other end of the phone, and it sounded genuine. She rarely snapped at me anymore during that period and any time after, rarely doffed the mask of the kinder, gentler persona that she seemed to have become, and the word "churlish," outmoded as it is, perfectly described how I felt as I held on to my distrust and anger.

And while I was still holding on to my resentments against her at that time, and I did keep my distance from her, I had begun to notice even before The Talk About The Blog that I was more amenable to the idea that it was not over yet, this Greek drama. I was starting to take a longer view of it and paying more attention to the notion of patience and letting things unfold in their own time. I had just completed some classes studying the *Tao Te Ching*, so that may have been part of it. And it's not like I hadn't heard the concept before.

All the way back to my Farraday days they were pounding into me the mantra "while this is how things are right now, it won't always be this way," trying any way they could to rewire my tendency to catastrophize all matters great and small. Then again, maybe I was starting to learn from my mother.

Whatever the case, the shift that began the night that I showed her the blog, the sense of progress and of leaving something behind in my wake, expanded as the days and weeks went by. I began to look at my mother through different eyes, and I had new thoughts and intuitions about her life. She was a much deeper person than I had given her credit for, because she had kept that part of herself well hidden, at least from me.

About this same time my mother started to reveal to me, directly and indirectly, aspects about her relationship with my father, and those insights further altered the way I looked at her. What she had given up in order to marry my father and the impact that choice had on her life became apparent when I invited a friend, Anna, to dinner with my mother. Anna was between our two ages and, as it turned out, from my mother's old neighborhood. After they reminisced about East 7th Street and Avenue J in Brooklyn, Anna asked my mother where she had gone to college. It was NYU, and she had graduated with a Bachelor of Science degree in Economics. My mother continued, "My

Economics professor was appointed to a big job in the government and asked me to come with him to Washington." Anna probed, and my mother said, with an inflection I couldn't identify, that she had already been engaged to my father, so she didn't go to Washington. She left it to Anna to supply the confirmation that of course my mother had made the right decision and look what a wonderful life she had made for herself with my father.

The story I had always heard, always from my father but without objection from my mother, was that my mother had gotten a good grade in Economics only because she sat in the front row and crossed her legs. My father was a chauvinist, a fact that escaped me until I was older and he began directing some subtle and not so subtle put downs at me. I wondered what it felt like, all those years, for my mother to play a supporting role when she so easily could have played the lead.

CHAPTER THIRTY-SIX

THE LAST PIECE OF THE PUZZLE

M Y FATHER. RELATIONSHIPS WITH men. Need. Addiction. Survival. Why Suzy became Suzy and stayed that way. Forgiveness.

I may not have gotten the order right, but those were the last pieces of the puzzle that I had to fit into the picture in order to make my psyche whole. Of course it had to come back to my father, that was such obviously unfinished business. For most of my life it was too hard to confront the defects in our relationship, so there was always something that cried for attention first, always "can't go there 'til I fix this."

Finally, one by one, the rest got more or less fixed, at least "close enough for government work," as my brother used to say, and by the time I reached my one year anniversary of leaving Alexander Hospital, I was left with that last puzzle piece: my relationships with men, which essentially meant my father. I still didn't want to face my issues about him, was reluctant to give up the anger, resentment, the disappointment, the need and the loss. I didn't know why I was so reluctant, only that I was.

I got a big clue on the night of my fortieth high school reunion in 2011. I had been looking forward to seeing everyone, joking via email for weeks in advance with friends with whom I had long last touch. Then I got the list of who had signed up for the event, and I stopped dead in my tracks. On the list was the name "Phillip Adams," and it brought back memories that I didn't want to think about, memories that could still make my face flush with embarrassment six years later.

Six years previously, I had just separated from Leo and had taken off on a quick trip to Atlanta as a distraction from the difficulties of the separation. I had grown up with Phillip there, and while I hadn't seen him for a while, we had been close and had kept in loose contact over the years, so I decided to look him up—lunch with a good looking, debonair bon vivant who was married and therefore "safe" seemed like a fun and harmless idea at the time. We went to lunch and the first thing I learned was that Phillip was single again, had gotten divorced since the last time we had spoken. In the space of twenty seconds I mentally morphed him from friend to lover to future husband to savior, not necessarily in that order. I was aware that I had clicked into some kind of compulsive hyperdrive, but put it down to sexual appetite and proceeded to pursue poor Phillip like the hounds of hell. Anyone who has seen the movie *Fatal Attraction* will understand when I say that if he'd owned a rabbit, that sucker would have been simmering in the pot before you could blink.

Phillip and I talked about having an affair, in a very adult way seemingly, though for me Suzy was signaling frantically behind the curtain to GET THIS DONE, because we NEED this, right? No one else was stepping up to the plate to help me stop spinning out of control and take charge of my fears. Phillip, God help him, had indicated that he cared about me, was interested in me, even attracted to me. Ultimately, Phillip decided that he would rather remain my friend than become my lover and risk losing the friendship, a very reasoned and mature response to the situation, just not the one that I wanted to hear, attached like a limpet to my phone. That's when I shifted from hyperdrive to some exponential factor of lightspeed. I called, emailed, cried, called back, emailed back, cried some more and left more messages, all the while insisting, in the face of Phillip's attempts to fend me off that he shared my yearnings, he just didn't realize it. I was there to help him over the hurdle, like it or not. Luckily, I poured out my woes to a mutual friend from high school, who somehow persuaded me to see the light—something about the way he saw this as an impending train wreck for all concerned finally made me pull my head out of my ass and see the boxcars hurtling towards each other and know that he was right.

I quit calling and emailing and after a while I quit crying as well and then forgot all about Phillip other than the occasional moment when he would flit in and out of my mind, no harm no foul. Until I saw his name on the reunion list. I freaked out a little, but I thought it was just from embarrassment—I wasn't used to being caught acting the fool and was nervous about seeing him again, unsure whether he would be judgmental or avoid me or, on the other hand, whether it would all be okay. As it turned out, it was better than okay, because I made myself walk right up to Phillip and give him a big hug, and he hugged me back and I could see that he wasn't put out with me anymore. We talked off and on through the evening, and he was just as delightful as I remembered, a wry smile, great wit and the kind of focus in conversation that made you feel like you were the most important person in the universe at that moment. I felt a little wistful watching him and thinking about him, even had a few shaky moments that I shrugged off, but I thought I was fine and felt pretty pleased about it.

Finally, the night was over and we said our goodbyes. Phillip and I gave each other a smile and a hug, he walked out one door and I took the elevator down to the parking lot where I had left my car. Out of the blue, I started to cry, at first just a few tears rolling down my cheeks. By the time I reached my car, they were pouring down my face and then I started crying in earnest, sobbing like a child. I cried all the way home, secretly cried myself to sleep (which was quite a trick, because I was at that time sharing my bed with a lover) and I cried when I woke up. I wiped away the tears to have sex, then got into the shower and burst into tears again. I cried all the way through the Sunday service I attended and then all the way to the house of a good friend who had been at the reunion, knew both Phillip and me from high school and knew the background story from six years before. I had nominated her to talk me through whatever the hell was going on.

I talked to her, I talked to Alex, the friend who had seen the train wreck coming all those years ago, I talked to other good friends and I talked to my therapist. After a couple of days, I understood what had happened. My reaction to Phillip had little to do with him as an individual and everything to do with what he represented to me—a man who cared about me, who looked at me like I mattered to him, who gave me the impression that if I needed help, I could count on him. In short, things that I had looked for from my father, but had not gotten, or at least not sufficiently. I still missed those things, was clearly still looking for them, and until I put this to rest, in my opinion it was going to screw up every relationship I was going to have with a man.

This was important to me because I had decided lately that I liked men, I really did. I loved my women friends, always did and always will, but, by God, men just seemed so cool, there was something about them (yes, even apart from sex). And I wanted one of my very own to hang out with, to go to Guns n' Roses concerts with, to listen to Open Mic/Spoken Word on Sunday nights at the Apache Café in Atlanta, to watch football with and to discover with me the world of things that I had held in abeyance while I filled the role of conservative lawyer Southern belle Jewish American Princess well-placed Atlanta/Norfolk Society minivan-driving mom.

CHAPTER THIRTY-SEVEN

❧

THE BIRTH OF SUZY
MARMALADE

F OR A WHILE I PLAYED with what I had learned from my encounter with Phillip and with the information I already knew about my father, gleaned more information from people who had known him well, let it all float around in my mind, wrote about it and turned that last puzzle piece around and around until I began to see a slot where it seemed to fit. I started with the premise that it was no accident that my food addiction had kicked back in for the first time in two years the night my father went into the hospital with a broken hip. I spent that night in his hospital room to make sure he was well looked after. As the night wore on, I got very antsy, until at 2:00 a.m. I went down to the all-night cafeteria and bought $12 of trail mix. Even at the hospital's exorbitant prices, that was a shitload of trail mix. I ate the entire bag in one sitting, without stopping to think about why I'd snapped after so long or what was really bothering me. From that day until the day I checked into Alexander, seven months later, and three months after my father died, I stayed on that road, rarely "clean" (odd terminology to apply to a food addiction, but anyone who is an addict knows that it is apropos). Clearly something had gotten triggered that night in the hospital, something related to my father that had sent me running, something that got triggered again at my high school reunion —and I needed to figure out what it had been.

I already knew from my years of therapy dissecting my food addiction what purposes the addiction served. What I had previously learned was reinforced at our sessions at Alexander, where the obvious addicts were openly lectured and I sat quietly by, taking it all in. The purposes of the addiction for me, as for most addicts, have been multifold and I can still say them in my sleep: to numb out uncomfortable feelings, to punish myself because I thought I deserved it, to feel anything at all rather than nothing at all and, in a twisted sense, to give myself nurturing that I had missed. So where did my relationship with my father fit into the pattern of my addiction?

I first had to separate my thoughts about my father from those about my mother. She had been my target for so long, it took some doing to put her to the side. But I did, and then I stepped back and did my best to assess my personal experience of my father objectively. With him, it wasn't how difficult or mean or rageful he was—not at all; he was a nice guy. I had known that even as a child. When I was really young, say age four to age ten or eleven, we adored each other, without reservation and without complication. I cannot overstate how pure and strong that love was, so strong that fifty years later, even with my Swiss cheese memory, I could still call up perfectly vivid memories of the feelings evoked when I raced up to him and threw my arms around him every night when he came home from work and his wrapping his arms around me in return. It was a love that was unthinking and untainted by any form of resentment or conflict, because he kept himself apart from the family conflicts, both because that was somewhat typical of a man of his era and because he detested confrontation of any kind.

The problem was that my father needed it to stay like that between us, because first of all, he was not equipped for the complications that inevitably came with my teenage years, and secondly, he had always been and continued to be surrounded by strong types who dominated him (father, older brother, wife), so the last thing he needed was for the one person he could count on to be easy suddenly to get difficult. On top of that, it's my guess that his own parents had not given him any kind of roadmap for profound interactions with family—as a middle child bracketed by a genius brother and baby sister, I don't think my father got all of the attention that he might have needed.

And thus was Suzy Marmalade the wide-eyed innocent born, as a placeholder for the child that my father needed to stay a child. I went along with it, voluntarily placing myself in suspended animation, because I needed him to stay the same as much as he needed that from me. I remained his little girl, called him "Daddy," lived on his money, which he gave generously, traveled with him and my mother as an adult child until I was thirty years old, and studiously avoided growing up. I will never forget being pulled over for an expired tag by a policeman when I was twenty-one, out of college and living on my own. I had no idea what he was talking about, that there was anything that had to be renewed annually and placed anywhere on my car, because my father had done all of that for me, so that it happened magically, without my participation or accountability. The cop gave me a ticket and walked away, shaking his head. I shook my head, too: what else did everyone else in the world know about the ordinary business of life that was news to me?

Quite a lot as it turned out, a shortcoming that challenged me up to and through law school. In my third year at law school, at twenty-eight years old, I learned for the first time that there were three systems of taxation in this country—income, gift and estate. That was a big surprise to me. I had never done anything other than sign the tax returns my father presented to me, and I'd been filing returns for years, because I'd had income from a relatively young age. By the end of law school, though, I had more or less caught up with the curve, a great accomplishment and a great relief.

I also got reacquainted, after a long dry spell, with the notion of men as friends and occasionally lovers in law school, and it blew me away. For the first time in my life I started to see men as people, not as tenuous cutouts who would go away if I didn't mold myself into their vision of me. That discovery was a great boon to me, but I didn't make any connection between those burgeoning relationships and the stagnant one I had with my father. I still viewed him through a child's eyes, unaware of the immaturity on both sides and how that might have the power to hurt one or both of us.

Something did, inevitably, happen, and I think it must have hurt my father quite a lot, though I didn't know it at the time. In 1985 I announced to him and my mother, after five years of practicing law at a major law firm in Atlanta, that I didn't enjoy the work and was quitting to move to New York to try to find a job in an art gallery. My mother's reaction was classic: "Good, you'll acquire a little town polish." My father's was extraordinary in how extreme it was—he was shocked, appalled, confused, and seemed to take it as a personal affront. He repeated over and over, how could I leave a good job that I had spent three years training for, without a job of any kind lined up to replace it? (Much later in life during the great recession of the second decade of the twenty-first century I became a convert to my father's way of thinking, but back then I was young and single; life was less circumscribed, and possibilities seemed worth the chance.) Then he went so far as to say, "I wish this had happened after I was dead." At that point I quit worrying about what he thought, because to me this was so over the top as to be ludicrous, and as such released me from any pangs of guilt or thoughts of taking him seriously. Despite his chagrin at my impending move, my father turned around and handed me a year's rent money. That made for a great year in Manhattan, but maybe I would have figured things out sooner if he hadn't done it. The gift of the money made me think that he was okay with my move after all, and I blithely moved to New York and didn't look back, not at him anyway.

I returned from New York after a year to marry Leo, and after that I started to notice a change in my relationship with my father—not all of a sudden, but bit by bit. I first started to notice that his generosity with money quickly dwindled. Okay, I could put that down to the fact that I was married now, plus a lawyer in my own right, so maybe in my father's mind Leo and I together as an income-producing unit were supposed to take over from him. I was surrounded by women whose fathers still lavished sums upon them and their spouses, but clearly my father had a different outlook. I made a mental note of it, a little puzzled, but took it reasonably well in stride, especially considering the rabid sense of entitlement that permeated my character at that time.

Then I noticed a big change of my own. After I was married and was around Leo's extended family for a while and saw how everybody called their father "Dad" or "Pops" or some other age-appropriate name, I became ashamed of calling my father "Daddy" and dropped the name like a hot potato, literally from one day to the next. I quietly gave it up—didn't tell him, didn't tell anyone, just stopped calling him that. Leaving me in a quandary, because nothing else fit. Just because I had decided not to call him Daddy

didn't mean our relationship was any different
or that some other name automatically fell into
place. "Dad" was out of the question, because he
didn't fit my definition of a "Dad." My idea of a
"Dad" was someone who was there to guide me in
the transition from teenager to adult and then to
young married woman, to give me sage advice as I
grew up. That was not my father. In fact, the more
he was called on to perform that task, the bigger
the gap between us grew, and the more I tried
to move on and grow up, the more it widened,
because he didn't know how to take the next step
toward which I was desperately fumbling. The
name my brother called my father, "Papasita"
didn't fit for me. It grew out of their particular
relationship that had nothing to do with me,
deriving as it did from the fact that they worked
together in matters involving Spanish-speaking
countries. Ultimately I adopted the name that
my children and niece called him—Papa—I
didn't even know how they spelled it for a long
time. To me, it was like a shorthand version of
"Hey, grandfather of my children." It always felt
strange, not having a real name to call my father
for the last thirty-five years of his life, especially
considering that I didn't have a "real" name for
my mother either.

As time went on, I noticed that I was occasionally
the recipient of my father's disapproval, sometimes subtly, sometimes openly and with cruelty,

especially when it had to do with my weight. Years later, after my father was dead and my mother read the earlier portions of this manuscript and saw the things I had written about him, she casually offered: "While you may have felt disappointed in your father, of course you were a great disappointment to him as well." (It was always a mistake to think that my mother had been completely defanged.) After I stopped reeling from the shock of that statement, I asked, "Why?" Her response: "Because you weren't thin enough and you quit practicing law."

I believed that up to a point. Appearances were very important to him and in his eighties he became almost anorexic in his approach to food. I knew that he had disapproved of me when I was overweight; he had said as much to me. I also knew that he had not taken my departure from practicing law well. He was a child of the Depression and certainly believed strongly in hanging on to a good job. But what I believed even more is that when I left for New York, it felt to him as if I had abandoned him and he never got over it. Suzy stayed in suspended animation for him for a long time, but when she stopped and moved on with her life, left the nest, first for New York and then by getting married, I think it felt like a great betrayal to him. How did I know these things without ever talking to him about them? Because that's how I would have felt, and we were two of a kind.

So when faced in that hospital room with the idea of losing my father, somewhere inside I had the feeling that I had lost him a long time ago, and that was a feeling that I needed to run from, wasn't ready to grapple with right then. That's when my addiction stepped in, to comfort me and soothe the pain that was more than I was prepared to feel. It took my writing it down in this book, with a considerable amount of resistance and a considerable amount of pain, to come to terms with my anger against and resentment of my father. It's a pity that we never made it back to the light, he and I, but after I wrote this down, I started to remember the good parts and to put the rest in perspective.

I started to remember who he had been as a person, and that in fact he had done some things that were not just good, they were spectacular, only they didn't have anything to do with me. For an easy-going, non-confrontational person, my father took an extreme and unwavering stand against segregation very early in the day. The family business opened a new plant in Atlanta sometime in the very late 1950s or early '60s, and the cafeteria was set up with long lunch tables in the way of all cafeterias since the dawn of time. My father noticed that the employees split up into groups—long tables filled with white people and long tables filled with black people. Mingling was nonexistent. It wasn't his habit to eat in the cafeteria, but once he saw what was happening, he went in there and made a point of having lunch with a group at one of the black tables. This was a pretty advanced and courageous act at that time, and he did it like he did most things, without fanfare and very much under the radar. But the precedent was set and it was clear that he meant it to be followed. He engaged in other acts opposing segregation, including the simple act of hiring black people as sewing machine operators rather than limiting their positions to the cleaning crew. It says how far America has really come that in the early 1960s it took nothing more than that to bring the Ku Klux Klan down on our heads, with threatening phone calls to my parents at home warning of all kinds of impending mayhem, including the threat of burning a cross on our lawn.

My father was also in the forefront of hiring the disabled, and I knew from personal experience that it wasn't just tokenism or lip service, because I worked on the factory floor in Atlanta the summer before I went to college. I watched his personal interactions with the disabled employees (as I recall they were mostly people who were developmentally disabled, "slow" we called it back then). He was completely natural and completely engaged, and there wasn't a shred of condescension or awkwardness in his manner. I couldn't have acted the way he did, not then and probably not now;

whatever he had in him that enabled him to do that so naturally did not pass down to me.

A lot of information about my father, including his stand against segregation, was in my father's obituary, but I was so mad at him at the time of his death that I couldn't look at it; I had to throw out the baby with the bath water for the moment. It was only through writing and talking with other family members who had known my father well that I was able to take a wider view of him and begin to let the good memories back in. And in time they did come, and I was able to come to terms with the fact that my father was neither a bad man nor a bad father. He and I had just missed the boat with each other in a way that was regrettable, and there was no help for that, it's just how it was.

CHAPTER THIRTY-EIGHT

COMEBACK

I N RETROSPECT, I REALIZE THAT other than
writing this book, the first thing that dug me
out of the pit was starting a job as a lawyer at the
end of August 2010, hired on a contract basis by
a law firm in response to one of the petitions I
had aimlessly flung into cyberspace during the
preceding months of joblessness like a Frisbee to
a blind dog. I found that I liked the job, which
came as no surprise to me, since practicing law
was the exact thing that I had fought against,
railed against, dreaded and made myself sick

over for years, weeping for my lack of passion and the hopelessness of a life without purpose. There's nothing like a few years at the bottom to loosen the stranglehold of drama: a paycheck is a mighty fine thing, a place to get up and go in the morning is not to be sneezed at, and exercising the old gray matter felt good. I remember the delicious sensation of my brain cells starting to stretch and bounce and dance in the corners. It had also come to my attention that one of the fundamental laws of the Universe is irony, so why wouldn't I like the precise thing that I thought I hated?

The further irony was that at that time I was regarded as the "rock" of my little group of new hirees, a direct quote from my employer. My co-workers called me the Zen queen, marveling at the evenness of my temperament. Four of us were hired at once to form a team of researchers and writers on a discrete project scheduled to last eight months to a year. Other than being all female, we were a diverse bunch, one more diverse than the rest, and her foibles often upset the other two. I played peacemaker, comedienne, old hand and go-between, with a little Suzy Marmalade thrown into the mix for my own amusement. I got it from the other end as well, called on by my employer to act as liaison and ground surveillance for the management of our little team. I sometimes felt like I was playing a part in a James Bond movie and never quite understood why a mundane legal assignment had turned into the equivalent of an espionage reality show. Regardless, the entertainment value was an unexpected plus and my role as lynchpin, given my state of mind just six months earlier, was gratifying.

The final irony was that the job hit my sweet spot by putting to use my skills as an internet detective, so long honed by my vintage handbag searches on Ebay and abortive day trading research in cultish chat rooms. I felt like a lawyer version of the Chinese chef, nothing had gone to waste, and I happily whiled away the hours, juggling search terms and word combinations like a cyberspace Julia Child exploring new pairings of herbs and spices. To cap it off, I got to write up my research in compact summaries, nothing too long, nothing too deadly, just enough to kick in a sense of pleasure at working with language.

Words are my grand passion, and the feeling that they produce in me is the closest I believe I will ever come to cosmic mysteries that are otherwise inaccessible to me, like the connection between mathematics and music. I have long been frustrated that that particular door is closed to me, familiar only as a half remembered dream from a former lifetime, and I stand in awe of people to whom the strands of that connection are brightly visible. These are the same people who fully understood

2001: A Space Odyssey and *What the Bleep* and *The Matrix* movies, all of which stumped me mightily, but I'll bet they don't know how to tell if a pearl is natural or artificial or whether the gold on the rim of a dinner plate is hand painted or part of a decal, all useless but entertaining skills which I acquired in my former life of grandeur.

I collect well-constructed, unusual and amusing sentences and get bogged down in books over a turn of phrase much in the way that the romance novels of my youth talked about a man getting distracted by a "well-turned ankle." Often in more recent times I have despaired of the survival of the well written word, given the prevalence of text exchanges such as the following between my daughter ("j") and a male friend ("m") late one Saturday night:

> j: sup
> m: sup
> j: what are you up to
> m: where you at
> j: where are you
> m: trinity
> j: really
> m: yea
> j: wow
> m: where you at
> j: not sure
> m: ok
> m: where are you (1:15am)

324

Really?? But I finally figured out that the twenty-somethings know how to switch gears perfectly well, they have just added textspeak to their repertoire of native languages. Still, I have yet to hear them match any of the favorites that I have gathered over the years. One such: "I fully intend, barring any unforeseen circumstances, to marry you." (How could I forget the delicious proposal of marriage that I received from Leo? Did I mention that we met in law school?) Another one, also courtesy of Leo, in correspondence from a lawyer on the other side of a deal: "In the absence of a more cooperative spirit from you, this matter is likely to become sharply adversarial, almost at once."

And how could I forget the man to whom I went for crystal repairs, a true craftsman and brilliant in many ways, but slightly off? I took a number of cracked and chipped vases to him to be repaired on a Tuesday, and received the promise that they would be ready the next day. I knew his m.o., so I gave him some time, waiting until the following Monday to return. When I went back in, he said that nothing was ready, and then issued the following immortal lines: "If you haven't received a call from me, you are armed with the knowledge that your items are not ready. However, your items have the potentiality to be ready at virtually any time, except right now." I fell down laughing as soon as I had cleared the threshold of his shop.

I have always been taken with the Word Jumble in the newspaper, and am perhaps the only person who has ever had a classified ad rejected by *The New York Times* because it was submitted in anagram form. It was in the personals, in 1985, in the days before Match.com and the like: "kesegni a nma htwi a snsee fo syterym how si ginkloo rof a manow tiwh lramisi steretin" (seeking a man with a sense of mystery who is looking for a woman with similar interest). The *Times* editors rejected it on the grounds that sexual content might be lurking in the jumble, exhibiting a lack of imagination, degree of censorship and conservative outlook that disappointed me greatly. I thought it was the perfect way for someone like me, a timid yet polished voracious reader and word junkie, to tease out a suitable prospect.

I knew that the happy confluence of work that utilized my pleasure in writing, stimulated my brain and provided me with a paycheck was helping me when I listened to a message on my cell phone at the end of the work day one afternoon and realized that I had overlooked my 5:00 p.m. appointment with my therapist. (A rare prize in the world of psychoanalysis, she thought it was a good sign, too.) It reminded me of Jim, my erstwhile boyfriend from the Big House. After reading a draft of this book, a friend pointed out to me that I had left his story hanging, never said where he went or what became of him. I had never felt so inclined, but after the lift I got from obtaining employment myself, the end of the story with him had more meaning for me.

Right after the "Oh, I guess you didn't commit suicide in my bathtub after all" scene and the phone call from our mutual friend at Alexander Hospital, Jim got dressed and ready to drive himself over to Kinnerd, his latest choice of curative retreat. He decided to check his email one last time before he left, and Praise Be, he had a message asking him to interview for a job in California. The change in Jim was immediate and dramatic. He practically danced with delight, sure that everything would be fine now: he loved his work and a job was all he needed. He had been out of work for six months and it had driven him into the ground, but now that was all over. He was out of the door five minutes later and I never saw him again, but I had little faith that that was all it would take to turn his crack-obsessed, chaotic life around.

Until I got my own job, and while not a panacea, it sure helped, so I had a little more hope and belief that this had also been the case for Jim. Because I think we suffered from a common ailment, one which I have seen in others in my group therapies and other therapies that I have attended: it is the tendency to succumb to a deep and abiding existential crisis, to a perceived failure to identify a passion or a purpose or a reason for being alive. We may fight against it, and fight hard, but many of us give in eventually, becoming jaundiced, bored and jaded, and eventually the depths of our not caring can become fathomless, frightening.

It was facing my fears, though, that I finally locked onto as the way out of the darkness and back to the light. I had become acquainted with a woman whom I like a lot and who shared some of my emotional issues. Frequently we would talk about solutions, but for a long time she seemed unready to try anything new, even though the old ways kept causing her pain. It frustrated me to watch her do the same hurtful things to herself, over and over, so I wrote her a letter, thinking that getting my feelings down on paper would release my frustration and maybe help her as well. When I re-read the letter, I realized that I had written it to myself:

> At the end of the day, what difference is it going to make that the things huddled inside of you were too frightening to look at? That you were too scared to bring them out and examine them? Do you think that God is going to say, "That's ok, I understand that you were too scared?" Do you think that you are going to get a prize and a pat on the head at the Pearly Gates and then your whole life will be retroactively

transformed to become worthwhile and fulfilling because God has compassion for your fear? I have no doubt that whatever eternal presence you believe in does feel boundless compassion for your fear and I am just as sure that once you're dead, it's rhetorical, at least for this lifetime. If you don't face your fears, you will stay stuck in the same spot, like being trapped in tar, and it is perfectly possible that you will die stuck in that exact same spot. Is that what you want? To live and die stuck in the same place, out of fear? I know that you are scared. And I am saying that it doesn't make any difference—in the end, you have to face your demons anyway. I'm not saying that you have to be brave all of the time or look at everything at once, but you have to tug on a string and start pulling it into the light. Otherwise you are going to live the rest of your life exactly as you are, whimpering a little every once in a while and complaining, but nothing is going to change and you will die feeling almost exactly as you do now. Do you want that?"

I don't. I spent twenty years getting fucked up, twenty years for it to calcify, twenty years undoing the damage, and, if I am lucky, I have twenty years more to run for the roses. I don't intend to waste them mired in fear.

This does not mean that I won't ever be afraid or feel despair again. In January of 2012, as I approached the two year anniversary of going into Alexander Hospital, I felt all kinds of bad—anxious, restless, couldn't sleep, all of the familiar and uncomfortable symptoms of psychic distress—only I couldn't figure out what was bothering me. Work was no more or less stressful than usual, my relationship with my mother and my kids was great, my pets were fine, all of my friends were healthy and there had been no upheavals like moving or anything else. It took me until the day before the anniversary date to pinpoint that it was the date itself that was troubling me, bringing back both bad memories and the fear that "it" (hospitalization) could happen to me again. I may have made out my adventures at Alexander to be entertaining, and while that was partly true, I was also using humor in self-defense. The truth is that I was well and truly traumatized by some of the things I saw there, and the resurfacing of those memories was not pleasant. I may have mentioned crack addicts at the hospital, but did I mention that one of them had laced the crack with strychnine (rat poison) and as a result had the most horrific boils on his arms where his tracks were? And I was being taken back to memories of Farraday as well. I have omitted that of the small group I knew in the ten weeks that I was there, three members killed themselves in the following year. One was a good friend. I still carry his number in my cell phone, as if by not deleting it I can keep him alive. Those were just some of the hard memories that were bubbling up, and I knew that I was going to need some help getting through and past the anniversary date that was bringing these things back to mind. I went into immediate action. I knew that it wouldn't be good for me to be alone with my thoughts all weekend, so I called in the troops and arranged to be active and with friends for much of the time. I saw three movies in two days, made an extra visit to my therapist, went to a doubleheader of my regular Sunday spiritual services and spent some hours writing. I did not run from the feelings nor did I wallow in them. I did a reasonably good job of actually feeling the feelings, always a challenge for me. And eventually the feelings passed, until the next round.

Everybody around me thinks that I have made it back, irrevocably, and so do I. All of the signs point to it: I have a stable job, stable relationships, stable reactions to stress, I look well and I feel well. I accept some things about myself that I never used to accept: that I am capable, self-reliant, strong, courageous, easy on the eyes and a real lady, to name but a few. I don't say "Yes, but" anymore when someone gives me a compliment. I acknowledge what I have accomplished and I don't make it small.

Having made all of that progress, having climbed back from the abyss not once, not twice, but three times, can I guarantee that I have made it back, always and forever? No. Why? Because the uncertainty of facing challenges without knowing the outcome is the human condition. I'm no different from anybody else. As a perpetual outsider, I find that reassuring. I understand the desire to have the question answered once and for all, definitively, no going back, no fingers crossed behind anybody's back: "Is she okay now?" Because it would be reassuring, wouldn't it, to know that this is a story of walking through the fire and coming out the other side? But it's not a one-time thing and then it's over. Walking through the fire is ongoing. I can say that I haven't done anything really unstable or unhealthy for going on two years now, if you don't count eating small bags of M&Ms. I go to work, I come home, I go on a bunch of ridiculous dates, I hang out with my friends and my mother, I play Trivia every Tuesday night (I suck), I go to rock concerts, I visit my children when I can and I travel as much as I can. I feel good most of the time and I laugh a lot.

I have always felt that, like Marlon Brando's character in *On the Waterfront*, I could have been, should have been, a "contender." My son once said, "I know that I was meant to do something important, because I've got flawless vision." It made me laugh, but at the same time I knew exactly how he felt. And finally, after getting sidetracked for the better part of my life, I know that I, too, am that. I am a contender.

THE END

ACKNOWLEDGEMENTS

I WOULD LIKE TO ACKNOWLEDGE the contributions by my editor, Lauren S. Cardon, brilliant professor of English currently at Tulane University, for making the necessary changes while making sure that my voice was never lost; Ulrike Guthrie for her superb proofreading talents, sparing me the ignominy of a book sprinkled with typos; Amy Weil, eminent appellate litigator by day and creative designer by night, for inspired advice about the design of this book; and Lane Carlock Howard and Brian Kurlander, writers of the play based upon the book, for their enthusiasm for the material and for sharing their creative process with me. I would also like to express my heartfelt appreciation to the people who formed the front line of my defense during the years of my unraveling. I find it extraordinary to recollect what they did for me.

There was Barbara, who made an overnight trip to visit me in Norfolk, Virginia in 2007. We stayed at a hotel and she signed a contract with me—I have forgotten what those contracts are called, but it is the opposite of a suicide pact—you sign it guaranteeing that you will take actions to promote your safety rather than hurt yourself in the event that you feel yourself at risk, like reaching out through phone calls or in extremis checking yourself into a hospital. What a burden that is to lay on someone, that they are bound in writing to be your last line of defense against taking your own life. This same friend called me every single day for three months that I am aware of, but it may have been more like six, before I went into Alexander and after I came out. Every day, just to give me something and someone to hold on to.

Another friend, Gretchen, showed up as my guide through the post-divorce meltdown, talking to me for hours and hours on the phone, day after day, patiently telling me the same things over and over and over again, the things that I did not want to but needed to hear. She told me that it was wrong to use my children as support, that I was the parent and they were supposed to look to me for stability, not vice versa. She said that I needed to get a job and stay busy and that nobody could put my life back together but me. I never believed that. I thought that somebody else was supposed to come along and do it. It took me years to pick up on the fundamental truth of Gretchen's admonition, but finally I did.

Cathie, my oldest friend, went through it all with me, not just for weeks or months, but for all of the years, and sometimes my pain and suffering hurt her so much that it made her cry, out of sympathy and out of helplessness. She is family, not just "like family," and because her own family is small, to lose me would have been to lose more than just a friend. Her worry was tangible, and, selfishly, that bolstered me. It reminded me on a daily basis that someone in the world cared whether I lived or died, giving me a feeling of substance that I desperately needed.

Liz used to drive down to Norfolk and stay with me on her way to South Carolina. She is among my most cerebral friends, and would talk it all through with me during these visits and over the phone, time and time again, why it hurt me so much to be alone, why I couldn't "snap out of it," how I needed to adjust my expectations of my family, and so on. Her own mother committed suicide when she was young, so I can't imagine what it was like for her to put her finger in the dike and hope that her friend wasn't going to go the same way.

Denise, my most recent friend in the front line, was all heart, and I do mean all heart. She would hold me and rock me while I cried, and beg me to think better of myself, tell me what a good and wonderful person I was and if she could believe that, why couldn't I?

Laura was a friend and a colleague at work, and was aware of my anguish, aware of the outlandishness of my days. She knew how often I had to lock my office door and lie down on the floor just to breathe, and then get up and negotiate a tough business deal, or leave work and go and collapse on the sofa at a therapist's office, then come back and draft a complicated legal document. One day, not too long before I checked into Farraday, I went in her office and said that I couldn't take it anymore, that I was going to quit (and voice a few choice opinions as well). She said, "Oh no, you're not, you are going home. I will do your work if I have to, but you are going to leave right now; I am not going to let you go in there and ruin your job, that's simply not going to happen." She meant it, and I went home and made it through that day and months to follow, until I couldn't.

Lam was my housekeeper who came once a week, and we became very close. I remember her sitting with me on the floor, holding me and rocking me, and pleading with me to believe that things were better than they felt to me.

Gabrielle was my yoga teacher, though truly more therapist than anything else. There is no limit to the things she tried, to the belief systems she laid out for me, the nutritional systems, the references to other practitioners she hoped could help. In the end it wasn't enough, but she helped stem a tide that otherwise would have swept me away entirely.

And finally, my brother. Of all the people not constructed for the kind of drama and pathos that made up the fabric of my existence in those years, it was he, a man of logic and mathematical precision. But he has another side, the side that takes care of people, and he was the single person who perceived the need for action and took it, first in helping me find and organize my sojourn at Farraday, and then doing the same at Alexander.

Those were All the King's Horsemen and All the King's Men. True, they couldn't put me back together again. But they held the pieces together, collectively a safety net sensed not just in my subconscious but often in the forefront of my mind, binding the fragments that were floating in the air into a patchwork whole, until I could hold the pieces together myself.

NOTES

1 Frank Zappa and the Mothers of Invention referred to "Suzy Creamcheese" as a vocalist and character on more than one album (including a song titled "Son of Suzy Creamcheese"). The name was also the title of a 1967 song by Teddy & His Patches, and the name of a Las Vegas clothing boutique in the 1960s and '70s, mentioned in the 1995 film *Casino*.

2 "Lucy in the Sky with Diamonds," featuring the lyric "tangerine trees and marmalade skies" appeared on the Beatles' 1967 album *Sgt. Pepper's Lonely Hearts Club Band* and was widely assumed to reference imagery from an LSD trip.

3 Slash with Anthony Bozza., *Slash*, New York: HarperCollins Publishers 2007, p. 256.

4   Fable of unknown origin (http://allaboutfrogs. org/stories/scorpion.html).

5   Kaminsky, Stuart, *Terror Town,* New York: Tom Doherty Associates, LLC 2006, p, 201.

6   Meyer, Stephenie, *New Moon,* New York: Little, Brown and Company 2006, p. 451.

7   Flores, Philip, Ph.D., *Addiction as an Attachment Disorder,* Maryland: Jason Aronson Publishers, Inc. 2004, p. 162, emphasis added.

8   Gaylin, Willard M.D., *Talk Is Not Enough: How Psychotherapy Really Works,* Little, Brown and Company 2000, p. 28.

9   Harris, Gardiner. *The New York Times* 6 March 2011, Sunday ed.:1. Print.

20683373R00187

Made in the USA
Lexington, KY
14 February 2013